THE FEAST OF FAITH

To
Stephen
With prayers
Father Elias
May 1991

ARCHBISHOP PAUL OF FINLAND

THE FEAST OF FAITH

AN INVITATION

to

THE LOVE FEAST OF THE KINGDOM OF GOD

Translated by Esther Williams

ST VLADIMIR'S SEMINARY PRESS
CRESTWOOD, NEW YORK 10707
1988

This publication was made possible
through the generosity of
ALEXANDER COLMAN
in memory of his beloved wife
EFTIHIA ARVANITI COLMAN

Library of Congress Cataloging-in-Publication Data

Paavali, Abp. of Karelia and All Finland, 1914-
  The Feast of Faith.

  Translation of: Uskon pidot.
  Bibliography: p.
  1. Lord's Supper (Liturgy). 2. Orthodox Eastern
Church Liturgy of St. John Chrysostom. 3. Lord's
Supper — Orthodox Eastern Church. 4. Orthodox
Eastern Church — Liturgy. 5. Suomen Ortodoksinen
Kirkko — Liturgy. I. Title.
BX355.P32   1988   264'.019036   88-11360
ISBN 0-88141-072-1

THE FEAST OF FAITH

PRINTED IN THE UNITED STATES OF AMERICA
BY
COSMOS PRINTING ASSOCIATES
NEW YORK, NY

CONTENTS

Translator's Note

The translation of the liturgical texts and prayers in this book is basically that of *The Divine Liturgy according to St John Chrysostom with appendices*, prepared by the Russian Orthodox Greek Catholic Church of America (New York, 1967; 2nd edition, 1977). Some alterations have been made to accord with the Finnish text of other translations: I.F. Hapgood's *Service Book*, 3rd edition (New York, 1956); *The Orthodox Liturgy* prepared by the Fellowship of Saint Alban and Saint Sergius (London, 1939); and *The Divine Liturgy Explained*, by Rev. Nicholas M. Elias, 4th edition (Athens, 1984).

The Bible quotations follow the Revised Authorized Version, with occasional use of the Revised Standard Version and the Authorized Version.

Quotations from Alexander Schmemann's *The Eucharist* are taken from Paul Kachur's translation published by St Vladimir's Seminary Press.

For the occasional quotations from the Fathers and early Church writings, the available English translations were used, though Greek and Latin sources were consulted as well.

We gratefully acknowledge our debt to the Orthodox Church in America and to all the translators and publishers of the above-mentioned sources.

Esther Williams

PREFACE

In the early Church several venerable and holy bishops wrote commentaries on the Divine Liturgy and the sacraments. St Cyril of Jerusalem, St John Chrysostom, St Ambrose of Milan, St Germanus of Constantinople are among them.

It is a great joy for me to welcome the present volume, entitled *The Feast of Faith* and written by one of the most respected and authoritative bishops in contemporary Orthodoxy, my dear brother in Christ Paul, Archbishop of Karelia and All Finland (who in late 1987 entered into retirement).

The most important feature of this work is its pastoral quality, the fact that it is addressed to the entire membership of the Church. By reading it, by learning from it, and by acquiring from it a real sense of what the various actions of the Divine Liturgy truly are, our priests and our laity will be able to make the Eucharist into the real center of the life of our parishes and of personal prayer life.

Archbishop Paul, in writing *The Feast of Faith,* was primarily addressing his own flock in Finland. However, the life of our sister Church in that country is, in many ways, similar to our experience in America. Here, as in Finland, Orthodox Christians constitute a minority, and are called to witness to their faith as missionaries. In a sense, each parish is called to become a mission, where people can "come and see that the Lord is good." Such a witness is impossible if the Orthodox community itself does not hear, does not know, does not understand the prayers, the gestures, the structure of the Divine Liturgy, when those prayers and gestures are nothing but a routine.

It is my conviction that whenever a parish begins to live the Divine Liturgy as the very mystery of faith, that parish will also grow spiritually and attract new faithful to the Church.

I recommend this book very highly to all Orthodox Christians in America. It is also my hope that through this book our non-Orthodox Christian brothers and sisters will better understand the sacred festal character of the Divine Liturgy. I express my gratitude to His Eminence, Archbishop Paul for authorizing its translation into English, and I wish him many years of health and spiritual fulfillment in the Lord.

†Metropolitan Theodosius
Primate
Orthodox Church in America

FOREWORD

I still recall the beginning of that letter word for word: "Please let me blow off a little steam. The apostles preached to the Jews and the pagans, but in the evening the adult Christians came together for a mystery service where the risen Lord Jesus was in their midst. For us — there is always preaching."

In the 1940's when that letter came, it was not usual for anyone to long for a mystery service.

Now, four decades later, many seekers have the same kind of longing as that teacher of classical languages who wrote the letter.

The phrase he used, "mystery service," was appropriate: as a linguist he apparently knew that, in the tradition of the Orthodox Church, the equivalent of the Western word "sacrament" is the word "mystery," derived from the Greek word for secret.

In the Orthodox Church the Liturgy, or Communion service, is just such a mystery service, the central part of which is called the Eucharist, a sacrifice of thanks.

The Liturgy is truly our heritage from the early Church. During the first three centuries the eucharistic prayers of the Liturgy were already crystallizing into permanent forms.

In later centuries the growing numbers of Christians, as well as new circumstances, brought about certain changes in the pattern of the Liturgy, but its eucharistic core has remained unchanged to this day.

When the Church was struggling against various heresies, the Liturgy came to include hymns and the Creed proper as permanent parts which expressed the right belief of the Church. The addition of these to the Liturgy shows the Church's basic view that prayer and faith belong together. According to Orthodox conception, faith does not consist of lifeless dogmas, definitions of belief, but of prayer, in which faith lives. Thus texts of the services, church poetry though they be, serve along with the Bible as sources for the Orthodox faith.

The Orthodox Liturgy is connected with the names of two fourth-century Fathers of the Church: Basil the Great and John Chrysostom. John Chrysostom was archbishop of the Byzantine center, Constantinople. This is one reason why the Liturgy bearing his name gradually displaced the forms of Liturgy originating in Jerusalem, Alexandria and Antioch and came to prevail throughout the Byzantine region. Later, as Christianity spread, this Liturgy also came to be celebrated in all the new Orthodox churches throughout the world. The Liturgy of Basil the Great is celebrated everywhere as well, but now only ten times a year.

When people look for the influence of Byzantine culture in Finland, for instance in Karelian architecture, how seldom they notice that the Orthodox Liturgy is the most genuine and spiritual expression of Byzantine culture here. In this Liturgy, at the same time, the message of the New Testament meets modern man. Ordinary methods of investigation, however, are unsuited to the study of the mystery service. It can be approached only on the inward path, through faith and experience.

This book is offered as a guide to those who want to become acquainted with the Orthodox Liturgy, even if only superficially. What will result from this acquaintance no longer depends on the guide, but on the Holy Spirit, which blows where it wills.

Our purpose is to try to shed light on the Liturgy in terms of its own texts, while at the same time taking notice of the most important changes which have taken place in the Liturgy in the course of its history and which help us to understand the present order of the Liturgy.[1]

Of course this work is also intended for Orthodox readers. The spiritual guidance and practical advice concerning the Liturgy in the notes and commentary and the appendix at the end of the book are meant especially for those who have joined the Church as adults.[2] Thus the book may also be regarded as an episcopal pastoral letter.

I have taken the liberty of dedicating my book to the memory of Archpriest Alexander Schmemann (1921-1983), Dean of St. Vladimir's Theological Seminary in New York. A researcher in liturgical theology, he inspired me to put into practice within my diocese some of the original principles of the Liturgy as a common act of the people of God. This book, too, is a natural result.

Archbishop Paul

NOTES

[1]The book may be brought to church if one wishes, and used to follow the Liturgy.

[2]Orthodox worship has its own special features, which it is well for the newcomer to know.

The worshippers generally *stand.* This is done not only out of respect for the Lord's house, but also because standing is the most natural position for man in his smallness as he prays to God in His holiness.

There are usually seats in the church for those who cannot stand during the service because of fatigue, illness, or disability.

In the Liturgy people sit during the sermon.

The sign of the Cross, depicting the symbol common to Christians, is integral to Orthodox worship. It is made with the right hand. The thumb and the first two fingers are placed together. These three fingers held together signify faith in the One Triune God: Father, Son and Holy Spirit. The last two fingers are bent against the palm to represent the two natures of Jesus, His divinity and His humanity. In making the sign of the Cross we put our hand to our forehead, inwardly asking God's blessing. Then we put our hand to our breast, that God may

The sign of the Cross

purify our hearts. Finally we touch each shoulder, first the right and then the left. Thus we ask for a blessing of our acts.

The sign of the Cross is both an unspoken confession of faith and the outward expression of inner prayer. In making the sign of the Cross a person prays with his whole being.

With the sign of the Cross we appeal to the redeeming Death of the Son of God; and with this sign of victory we banish the evil thoughts and feelings that creep into our hearts.

When a prayer in the service is spoken or sung three times, as for example "Holy God," the sign of the Cross is also made three times in the Name of the Holy Trinity.

The sign of the Cross is always, with few exceptions, associated with a bow to the object of the prayer, the invisibly present God. First we peacefully make the sign of the Cross and then we bow.

Censing came into the Christian Church from Old Testament worship. Its meaning is expressed in the words of a psalm: "Let my prayer arise in Thy sight as incense" (Ps 141:2).

As he blesses the censer, the priest prays: "We offer Thee incense, O Christ our God, for an odor of spiritual fragrance. Receive it upon Thy heavenly altar, and send down upon us in return the grace of Thine all-holy Spirit."

When censing in the church the priest or deacon turns toward both the icons and the people in the church. Man is an icon created in the image of God, although sin has tarnished this image. The censing is directed to this image of God in both the icons and the people present. Those being incensed respond humbly with a bow, showing that they need the grace of the Holy Spirit, without which there is no real prayer.

The censing is done with a vessel called a censer. It is a covered cup suspended on chains and containing glowing coals and incense. As he censes, the priest or deacon swings the censer cross-wise and bows simultaneously. There are also small censers for home use.

The priest *blesses* with his right hand, his fingers forming the Greek initials for Jesus Christ, IC XC. This form of blessing reflects the view of the Orthodox Church that the apostolic priesthood is Christ's priest-hood, and it is as its bearer that the priest gives the blessing.

When the priest blesses the people, they all bow in acknowledgment of the blessing.

When a believer meets a priest outside the church and asks for a blessing, he puts his right hand over his left, palms upward. After blessing him with the sign of the Cross, the priest lowers his hand for the believer to kiss as a sign that the blessing comes from Christ

The priest's blessing

Himself through this bearer of Christ's priesthood.

On meeting or taking leave of a bishop, the believer asks for blessing and kisses the bishop's hand in the same way as with a priest. As with the priest, it is not a question of the person, but of the grace of Christ's priesthood given to those who have received the apostolic priesthood.

The lighting of candles is an Orthodox custom common to all parts of the world. In the Karelian tradition a church candle is called a "tuohus," meaning "taper." A person who buys a taper places it, as his kindled prayer, on the candle stand in front of an icon. The taper, made of pure beeswax, reminds him that his prayer must be burning and come from a pure heart. After placing his taper on the candle stand and praying before the icon, the person usually kisses the icon, thus having physical contact with holiness. This holiness is not in the material, in matter, but in what the material icon reveals and makes present.

Each person decides for himself before which icon or icons he will place his taper. In every church there is an iconostasis, an icon screen, between the sanctuary and the body of the church. The function of the icons on the iconostasis is to mediate the connection between the heavenly, rejoicing part of the Church and the part of the Church still struggling on earth. On one side of the Royal Doors at the center of the iconostasis is an icon of Christ, and on the other an icon of the Mother of God. Most people place their tapers before these icons, but there are many other icons in the church which are particularly venerated by members of the congregation. There is also a low table in the church for the remembrance of the departed. On it is an icon representing the theme of Golgotha. Lit tapers are placed on this table by those who wish to remember their departed relatives and friends in this way, saying a prayer for them: "Give rest, O Lord, to the souls of Thy servants."

Tapers may be put in front of icons at any time, but people usually do so when they first enter the church.

It should be noted that, during service, non-Orthodox persons are not required to follow the Orthodox custom indicated above. They are, however, free to do so if they wish. For instance, they may make the sign of the Cross, bow, light tapers, and go with the others at the end of the Liturgy to kiss the Cross or — in the Vigil — the Book of the Gospel. Only participation in Holy Communion is restricted to members of the Orthodox Church. The reason for this is made clear in the explanation of the Liturgy and the conclusion of the work.

A SHORT INTRODUCTION
TO THE LITURGY

"Heaven on Earth"

The Orthodox Liturgy, like the Mass in the Catholic Church, is always a communion service and not simply an altar service in general.

In the Liturgy the congregation partakes of the "bread which came down from heaven" — Holy Communion (Jn 6:41). It has been said that at Communion "heaven comes down to earth." Each person experiences the closeness of the Kingdom of God according to his own powers.

Each receives Communion for the remission of his own sins and unto life everlasting. But the Liturgy is not limited to the fact that at Communion individual members of the Church receive forgiveness of their sins. The Liturgy is an ever-repeating experience by the whole congregation, the people of God, of the love of God and the reality of salvation. The Divine Liturgy will bear witness of this to the world "until he comes," until the Second Coming of Christ (I Cor 11:26).

Commentary: *In the explanation of the Liturgy the term "people of God" is often used. It refers to both the clergy and the members of the congregation. This term is based on the teaching of the New Testament concerning the members of the Church as the people of God: "But you are a chosen generation, a royal priesthood, a holy nation, His own special people, that you*

15

may proclaim the praises of Him who called you out of darkness into His marvelous light; who once were not a people but are now the people of God, who had not obtained mercy, but now have obtained mercy" (I Pet 2:9-10). According to this, all who have been baptized and received the gift of the Holy Spirit are the same people of God.

It is worth noting that the concept of laity is known in neither the New Testament nor the texts of the services. The Liturgy speaks either of the learners who do not yet belong to the Church or of the faithful and the saints. The term "layman" came into use when the people of God began to be divided sharply into two groups, those ordained to the priesthood on the one hand, and those not ordained, the laity, on the other. At the same time the clergy were identified with the Church and the laity with the world. In this way, an excessive clericalism developed in the Church, and the nonordained members of the people of God were labeled laymen, incompetents. And indeed they became ignorant about matters of the Church, and passive as well. In reality, all members of the Church who have been chrismated, anointed by the Holy Spirit, are equally members of the people of God. The prayers of all are offered in the Eucharist, and the petition for the gift of the Holy Spirit is made for all in the same way.

From Early Times to the Present Day

In the early centuries of the Church, both the faithful, the members of the Church, and the catechumens, who were preparing to receive Holy Baptism, were present during the first part of the Liturgy. The reading of the Word of God and teaching had a central place in this part of the Liturgy. After the sermon, prayers were said for those who were preparing for Baptism asking "that He may reveal to them the gospel of righteousness" and "unite them to His Holy Catholic and Apostolic Church." Then the catechumens were dismissed.

Today, the Liturgy still has the same structure as in early Christian times. Accordingly, the first part of the Liturgy is called the Liturgy of the Learners, or Catechumens, and the last part is called the Liturgy of the Faithful.

Liturgy - Eucharist

The Liturgy of the Faithful consists of giving thanks to God for His creation and for all His saving acts, and of Communion.

Thanks are given in the form of a verbal thank-offering, which is the meaning of the word "eucharist." In the Eucharist, the sacrifice on the Cross at Golgotha and the verbal thank-offering by the congregation meet in a hidden way; thus in the Eucharist the faithful become participants in the reconciliation and the new life which Christ gave to the world by His Death and Resurrection.

The word "eucharist" is often used as an equivalent for the word "liturgy." More precisely, however, the Liturgy is the whole Communion Service, which contains a specific pattern, texts and actions; and the Eucharist is the part of the Liturgy consisting of the eucharistic prayers, known as the eucharistic canon. The word "eucharistic" is also often used when the spiritual, hidden essence of the Liturgy is meant.

Commentary: *Not even the most precise description of the Liturgy can fully explain the inner, spiritual*

*essence of the Eucharist. It is a mystery just as the
"mystery of God" is in Christ (Col 2:2).*

First, it is a spiritual mystery because man is not
capable of attaining the whole truth only through logical
thought. The path of reason leaves him without any
vision of the spiritual reality which also exists. The
spiritual realm is just as much a reality as the world
perceived by our senses, and often it is even revealed in
visible symbols.

In order to perceive spiritual reality — or any reality
in general that transcends the rational — spiritual senses
are needed. This also applies to the world of church
services, and particularly to the Eucharist. The Eucharist is a mystery on many levels.

Every believer's experience of the mystical reality of
the Eucharist depends on his own personal faith. Never-
theless, it is not simply a matter of each person's
subjective, emotional experience. Theologically, one
can speak of the same objective experience common to
all.

In his explanation of the mystery of the Eucharist
Alexander Schmemann says:

> ...the liturgy is served on earth, it is accomplish-
> ed in heaven. But most important is the fact that
> what is accomplished in heaven is already ac-
> complished, already is, already has been accom-
> plished already given. Christ has become man,
> died on the cross, descended into hades, arisen
> from the dead, ascended into heaven, sent down
> the Holy Spirit. In the liturgy, which we have
> been commanded to perform "until he comes,"
> we do not repeat and we do not represent—we
> ascend into the mystery of salvation and new

life, which has been accomplished once, but is granted to us "always, now and forever and unto ages of ages." And in this heavenly, eternal and otherworldly eucharist Christ does not come down to us, rather we ascend to him. (The Eucharist. Sacrament of the Kingdom, *St Vladimir's Seminary Press, 1988, p. 221*).

The Church — a Eucharistic Community

The essential nature of the Orthodox Church and its Communion Service can be described with three words of Greek origin: *ecclesia, leitourgia, eucharistia.*

The word *ecclesia* expresses the idea of the Church as the people of God, called together again and again to assemble in one place. When we ask why the people of God gather again and again, the answer is provided in the word *leitourgia*, which in Greek originally meant a public service.

When we further ask what is the common service for which the people of God are called together again and again, the question is answered in the word *eucharistia:* they come together to give thanks to God, to bring Him a thank-offering.

Although the Church has its own historical foundation, form and order, it is not essentially a rigid body, but a community which is always in living motion. It becomes the Church each and every time the people of God assemble to celebrate the Eucharist together. And in this coming together each of the faithful becomes what he is through Baptism — a member of the Church in the full sense of the word, a member of the Body of Christ. "Now you are the Body of Christ, and members individually" (I Cor 12:27).

The Celebrants of the Liturgy

These three factors, *ecclesia*, *leitourgia* and *eucharistia*, are essential and interdependent.

The apostolic succession is a guarantee of the authenticity of the *ecclesia*, or Church. The validity of the Eucharist too rests on this. The bishop and martyr Ignatius, a direct successor of the apostles, wrote to the Christians at Smyrna: "Let that Eucharist be looked upon as well established which is either offered by the bishop or by him to whom the bishop has given his consent" (8:1).

Just as important as the leadership of a bishop or a priest to whom he has given authority, is the conscious participation of the congregation, the people of God, in the Liturgy, a service which must be celebrated in common. The priest, who himself belongs to the people of God, "standing at the front" offers the people's common prayers to God, and the people confirm his words with their own amen.

The Liturgies of Chrysostom and Basil

The most common communion service in the Orthodox Church is the Liturgy of St John Chrysostom (†407). The Liturgy of St Basil the Great (†379), celebrated ten times a year, is similar in pattern, but the texts of its prayers differ in some places from those of Chrysostom's Liturgy.

Commentary: *A distinctive feature of the Liturgy of Basil the Great is that it has longer Eucharistic prayers than the Liturgy of Chrysostom. The Liturgy of Basil the Great is celebrated each year on the following occasions: 1) the feast day of St Basil the Great (January*

1); 2) *the Eve of the Nativity of Christ (Christmas) and the Eve of Epiphany (or the day of Epiphany if it falls on a Sunday or Monday, in which case the Liturgy of John Chrysostom is celebrated on the Eve); 3) the five Sundays of Lent; and 4) Thursday and Saturday of Holy Week.*

Another Liturgy, differing from these two and originating in Jerusalem, is also known in the Orthodox Church. This is the Liturgy of the Apostle James, brother of the Lord. It is celebrated on his feast day, October 23.

There is still a fourth form of Liturgy in use in the Orthodox Church: the Liturgy of the Pre-sanctified Gifts. It is referred to as the Lenten Liturgy because it is celebrated only during Lent (on Wednesdays and Fridays, on Thursday of the fifth week of Lent, and on Monday, Tuesday and Wednesday of Holy Week). This Liturgy, connected with the name of the Roman Pope Gregory Dialogos, is celebrated in the evening and begins with Vespers. The Eucharist is not celebrated at this Liturgy, but Communion, consecrated during the previous full Liturgy, is distributed.

The remarks in this book are based on Chrysostom's Liturgy.

Although the historical division of the Liturgy into two parts, the Learners' Liturgy and the Liturgy of the Faithful, is still apparent in the liturgies of our time, the content of the Liturgy is divided here into seven parts for the sake of clarity:

1. The Beginning of the Liturgy — the Enarxis
2. The Liturgy of the Word
3. The Great Entrance

The Royal Doors are opened, the Liturgy begins

THE DIVINE LITURGY
OF OUR HOLY FATHER

JOHN CHRYSOSTOM

**The text and order of the Liturgy follow the
handbook published in 1985***

THE BEGINNING OF THE LITURGY

The entire Liturgy, like all the other services of the
Orthodox Church is continuous prayer.

Commentary: *Before the beginning of the Liturgy
the service of Matins is celebrated in the church. If
Matins has already been performed, the Third Hour is
read before the Liturgy. The psalms and prayers of the
Hour prepare the congregation for participating in the
Liturgy which is about to begin.*

*During the reading of the Third Hour is a suitable
time for people in the congregation to place candles
before the icons. The priest, alone or with a deacon, in
the sanctuary, performs the "Liturgy of Preparation,"
also known as the Proskomede. Here, in symbolic biblical terms, bread and wine are prepared for the Eucharist.*

*The Proskomede is performed in the sanctuary at a
side table commonly called the Table of Oblation. The
Table of Oblation proper, on which the eucharistic
sacrifice of thanks is offered, is the Holy Table in the
center of the sanctuary.*

---

*) The 1985 Finnish handbook is used in two Finnish dioceses, where
the metropolitans have approved its use (EW).

*At the Proskomede five loaves
of bread are used. They are
called* prosphora *(prosphora
is Greek for sacrifice). A prosphora is a small wheat bread
made with one part superim-
posed on the other, symbolizing the two natures of Christ,
His divinity and His humanity. Before being baked, the
bread is stamped with a seal*

Church bread

*consisting of a cross and a monogram for Jesus Christ:
the initials IC XC, and the Greek word NIKA, which
means "He conquers."*

One of the five prosphoras *is chosen as the communion bread proper. A cube-shaped piece is cut from
this bread with a small knife shaped like a lance. This
bread is called the Lamb. Particles are taken from the
other prosphoras in honor of saints and the living and
departed who are being commemorated. The Lamb
and the particles are placed on the communion plate,
called the* diskos, *where they represent the Church,
Christ surrounded by His saints. At the end of the
Liturgy, after Communion has been distributed, the
priest puts the remaining small particles into the chalice.
As he does this the priest says: "Wash away, O Lord, the
sins of all those remembered here, by Thy precious
Blood; through the prayers of Thy saints."*

*After the Proskomede the priest or deacon incenses
the sanctuary, the iconostasis and the whole church.*

*The iconostasis is intended not to separate the altar
from the body of the church but to build a connection
between the earthly and heavenly congregations. The*

icons on the icon screen and elsewhere in the church are a visible sign of contact through prayer.

When the Proskomede is finished, the priest and deacon stand before the altar table and read the prayers which lead into the Liturgy.

Lifting up his hands (cf. I Tim 2:8), the priest asks the Holy Spirit to come upon the celebrants: "O Heavenly King, the Comforter, the Spirit of Truth who art everywhere and fillest all things, Treasury of Blessings, and Giver of Life: Come and abide in us, and cleanse us from every impurity, and save our souls, O Good One."

The priest then twice recites the song of praise sung by the angels on Christmas night to proclaim the glory of God and His good will to men: "Glory to God in the highest; and on earth peace, good will towards men" (Lk 2:14).

Finally, the priest prays that he too may proclaim God's praise during the holy sacrifice of thanks: "O Lord, open Thou my lips and my mouth shall show forth Thy praise" (Ps 51:15).

At the conclusion of the prayer the deacon says to the priest: "It is time to begin the service to the Lord. Bless, Master" (cf. Ps 119:126). The priest blesses him, and the deacon leaves the sanctuary to take his usual place in front of the iconostasis and says: "Bless, Master." The priest then begins the Liturgy proper by intoning the opening blessing.

When the time comes to begin the Liturgy, the Holy Doors at the center of the iconostasis are opened, and the Kingdom of God is proclaimed from the altar. The priest at the altar table pronounces the initial blessing.

Blessed is the Kingdom of the Father, and of

the Son, and of the Holy Spirit, now and
ever and unto ages of ages.

Praise is the highest form of prayer, in which man
forgets himself. Indeed, the redemptive act has already
taken place, and God through Christ has revealed
Himself as the Holy Trinity. The Kingdom of the Father,
Son and Holy Spirit is a reality for those who have been
baptized through water and the Spirit into membership
in the Body of Christ, the holy Church.

On hearing the priest's initial blessing, the congregation, often represented by the choir, joins in this praise
of the Kingdom of God by singing "Amen," which
means "It is truly so."

Thus a dialogue begins between the priest or deacon and the congregation, and this continues throughout the Liturgy.

The initial blessing is followed by the Great Litany,
a responsive prayer consisting of the general prayers of
the Church. There follow three antiphons or respon-
sorial hymns, with a prayer for each antiphon read by
the priest.

During the singing of the third antiphon the Gospel
book is carried in solemn procession from the side
door of the sanctuary, down the side of the church to
the door, and from there back to the Holy Table. The
first part of the Liturgy concludes with songs about the
feast of the day or the ascetic struggle of the saints
whose memory is kept on the day.

+

In peace let us pray to the Lord.
For the peace from above and for the salvation

of our souls, let us pray to the Lord.
For the peace of the whole world,
for the welfare of the holy churches of God,
and for the union of all, let us pray to the Lord.
For this holy house and for those who enter with
faith, reverence and the fear of God,
let us pray to the Lord.
For our Patriarch. . . , our Archbishop. . . .,
for our Metropolitan. . . (Bishop. . .),
for the honorable priesthood, the diaconate in
   Christ,
for all the clergy and the people,
let us pray to the Lord.
For the President of our country, for all civil
authorities, and for the armed forces,
let us pray to the Lord.
For this city (village, holy monastery),
for every city (village) and country and for the
faithful dwelling in them, let us pray to the Lord.
For seasonable weather, for abundance of the
fruits of the earth, and for peaceful times, let us
pray to the Lord.
For travelers by land, by sea, and by air; for the
suffering; for captives and their salvation, let us
pray to the Lord.
For our deliverance from all affliction, wrath,
danger and necessity, let us pray to the Lord.
Help us, save us, have mercy on us, and keep us,
O God, by Thy grace.

This Great Litany or responsory prayer, in which
the choir answers the deacon or priest with the prayer
"Lord, have mercy," is also called the Litany of Peace.

It begins with a prayer for the peace of our souls and of the whole world. This peace comes "from above," it is the peace of the Kingdom of God in the Holy Spirit (Rom 14:17).

Each litany ends with a prayer in which we are urged to follow the example of the saints and, asking for their intercessions, to commit ourselves completely to Christ, for Christ is "our peace" (Eph 2:14).

> Commemorating our most holy, most pure,
> most blessed and glorious Lady, Theotokos
> and ever-virgin Mary with all the saints, let us
> commend ourselves and each other, and all
> our life unto Christ our God.

After the choir responds "To Thee, O Lord," the priest reads the antiphon prayer:

> O Thou who hast given us grace
> with one accord to make our common suppli-
> cations unto Thee, and hast promised
> that when two or three are gathered together
> in Thy Name Thou wouldst grant their requests.
> Fulfill now, O Lord, the petitions of
> Thy servants as may be expedient for them;
> granting us in this world the knowledge of
> Thy truth, and in the world to come,
> life everlasting.
> — For unto Thee are due all glory, honor,
> and worship: to the Father, and to the Son,
> and to the Holy Spirit,
> now and ever and unto ages of ages.

This prayer is read by the priest on behalf of the people who have gathered in the Name of God.

Like nearly all the prayers, this prayer ends in an expression of praise, a doxology. Praise is given to the Holy Trinity, since all the Persons of the Trinity take part in man's salvation. The choir sings "Amen" as an ending to the doxology.

Commentary: *This prayer, which in the previous order of the Liturgy was the third antiphon prayer, was moved in the 1985 Finnish handbook to first place. It speaks of being "gathered together," and it was read at the beginning when the Liturgy started with the entrance, the present Little Entrance.*

If this prayer is not read aloud to the congregation, it indicates that the Liturgy is being celebrated in the older fashion, with the priest reading the prayers "secretly," or to himself (see pages 64-7).

The first antiphon, taken from Ps 103, follows:

> Bless the Lord, O my soul!
> Blessed art Thou, O Lord!
> Bless the Lord, O my soul!
> And all that is within me, bless His holy name:
> Bless the Lord, O my soul!
> And forget not all His benefits!
> Who forgives all your iniquity,
> who heals all your diseases!
> Who redeems your life from the pit,
> who crowns you with steadfast love and mercy!
> The Lord is compassionate and merciful,
> long suffering and of great goodness!
> Bless the Lord, O My soul!
> Blessed art Thou, O Lord!

The term antiphon points to the fact that the verses

of the psalm are intended to be sung alternately by two choirs, or even two singers.

The antiphon "Bless the Lord, O My soul" is sung on Sundays, on lesser feasts, as well as at the after-feasts of the major feasts. On major feasts and week-days, the antiphons are taken from other psalms which express the theme of the day.

> "Again and again in peace let us pray to the Lord."

The deacon's repeated exhortation emphasizes the continuity of prayer and introduces the second anti-phon prayer, which the priest reads:

> O Lord our God, Thy power is beyond compare. Thy glory cannot be understood. Thy mercy cannot be measured. Thy love for man cannot be expressed. Look down on us and on this holy house with pity, O Master, and impart the riches of Thy mercy and Thy compassion to us and to those who pray with us.
>
> — For Thine is the majesty, and Thine are the Kingdom and the power and the glory: of the Father, and of the Son, and of the Holy Spirit, now and ever and unto ages of ages.

The choir sings "Amen" to conclude the doxology and then sings the second antiphon. On Sundays, it consists of verses from Ps 146:

> Praise the Lord, O my soul!
> I will praise the Lord as long as I live;
> I will sing praises to my God while I have being,
> The Lord will reign forever;
> Thy God, O Zion, to all generations.

A doxology to the Holy Trinity and the hymn "Only-begotten Son" conclude the second antiphon.

> Glory to the Father and to the Son
> and to the Holy Spirit
> now and ever and unto ages of ages. Amen.
> Only-begotten Son and immortal Word of God
> who for our salvation willed to be incarnate
>   of the holy Theotokos and ever-virgin Mary
> who without change became man and was
>   crucified
> who is one of the Holy Trinity, glorified with
>   the father and the Holy Spirit:
> O Christ our God, trampling down death
>   by death, Save us!

This hymn, which expresses the Church's faith in the divinity and humanity of Christ, was introduced by the Byzantine Emperor Justinian.

Commentary: *The 1985 handbook also provides a separate order for the Baptismal Liturgy. The Liturgy begins with the opening blessing and the troparion "Only-begotten Son," just as in Jerusalem in the seventh century.*

The Little Entrance takes place during the singing of "Only-begotten Son," and the Great Litany follows. Holy Baptism and Chrismation are then performed. After this Liturgy continues in the customary way with the singing of "As many as have been baptized into Christ."

> Again and again in peace let us pray to the Lord.

The choir responds with "Lord, have mercy." and
the third antiphon prayer follows:

> O Lord our God,
> save Thy people and bless Thine inheritance.
> Preserve the fullness of Thy Church.
> Sanctify those who love the beauty of Thy house;
> glorify them in return by Thy divine power,
> and forsake us not who put our hope in Thee.
> — For Thou art a good God and lovest mankind,
> and unto Thee we ascribe glory:
> to the Father, and to the Son, and to the
>   Holy Spirit,
> now and ever and unto ages of ages.

The third antiphon on Sundays is the "Beatitudes":

> In Thy Kingdom remember us, O Lord,
> when Thou comest in Thy Kingdom.
> Blessed are the poor in spirit,
> for theirs is the Kingdom of Heaven.
> Blessed are those who mourn,
> for they shall be comforted.
> Blessed are the meek,
> for they shall inherit the earth.
> Blessed are those who hunger and thirst after
> righteousness, for they shall be filled.
> Blessed are the merciful,
> for they shall obtain mercy,
> Blessed are the pure in heart,
> for they shall see God.
> Blessed are the peacemakers,
> for they shall be called the sons of God.
> Blessed are those who are persecuted for

righteousness' sake, for theirs is the Kingdom
  of Heaven.
Blessed are you when men shall revile you
and persecute you, and shall say all manner of
evil against you falsely for my sake.
Rejoice and be exceedingly glad,
for great is your reward in heaven.

The Beatitudes contain Christ's own teaching: they
are not merely Old Testament psalms. While they are
sung the Little Entrance takes place. The Gospel book
is taken from the side door of the sanctuary, carried
down the side of the church to the front door, and
from there up to the center aisle back to the solea or
altar platform. The people turn toward the procession
and venerate the Word of God by crossing themselves
and bowing. On the solea, the priest blesses the procession saying: "Blessed is the entrance of Thy saints
always, now and ever and unto ages of ages." Then the
deacon lifts up the Gospel book, which contains divine
wisdom, and says:

Wisdom! Let us attend!

The procession with the Gospel book, which precedes
its proclamation, portrays the appearance of the risen
Christ Himself and the fulfillment of His promise:
"Where two or three are gathered in my name, there
am I in the midst of them" (Mt 18:20).

The congregation bows to the risen Christ and
sings to Him:

Come, let us worship and fall down before
  Christ,
who rose from the dead. O Son of God, save
us who sing to Thee: Alleluia!

The deacon places the Gospel book on the Holy Table in the sanctuary, where the Word of God, symbolic of Christ Himself, should be.

Commentary: *In some Greek monasteries the book is not taken straight to the Holy Table after the Entrance but is left on the lectern. It would be more logical not to take it to the altar until after the reading of the Gospel — as is done in the Liturgy of James.*

The celebrating clergy follow the Gospel book into the sanctuary. Symbolically, this means that Christ takes all the followers of His Word into the Kingdom of God, represented in the Liturgy by the sanctuary. In this sense, the whole people of God moves towards God's Kingdom.

Immediately after the Little Entrance, the Church remembers those holy followers of Christ's Gospel who are commemorated that day. The hymns called *troparia* and *kontakia* praise the struggle of the saints and the grace of the Holy Spirit manifested in them. On feast days, these hymns express the content of the feast.

Troparia and *kontakia* are changing, variable parts of the Liturgy. They reveal the seasons of the church year, such as Lent, the Easter season, or saints' days.

The *troparia* and *kontakia* are sung in any of eight tones, which follow various liturgical cycles. For example, the Sunday *troparion* in the first tone is the following:

> When the stone had been sealed by the Jews;
> while the soldiers were guarding Thy most
>   pure Body;
> Thou didst rise on the third day, O Savior,

granting life to the world. The powers of heaven
therefore cried to Thee, O Giver of Life: glory
to Thy Resurrection, O Christ!
Glory to Thy Kingdom!
Glory to Thy dispensation,
O Thou who lovest mankind.

The deacon reads the Gospel

THE LITURGY OF THE WORD

The reading of the Word, the books of the Bible, has been integral to the Liturgy from the beginning, as is evident from all the early sources.

Just as Christ, the Word of God, the Logos, "became flesh and dwelt among us" (Jn 1:14), so also the Word that is heard becomes flesh in the assembled congregation. In Communion, Christ the Word becomes our life.

Thus the Word is the direct source of the Eucharist and is fulfilled there.

The Liturgy of the Word includes the song "Holy God," the Epistle, the Gospel, and the instruction through the sermon.

+

The song "Holy God" is introduced by a prayer read by the priest:

> O holy God; who dost rest in the saints;
> who art hymned by the Seraphim
> with the thrice-holy cry,
> and glorified by the Cherubim,
> and worshipped by every heavenly power. . .
> . . .Thyself, O Master, accept even
> from the mouth of us sinners the thrice-holy
> hymn, and visit us in Thy goodness.
> Forgive us every transgression,

both voluntary and involuntary.
Sanctify our souls and bodies,
and enable us to serve Thee in holiness
all the days of our life. . .
— For holy art Thou, O our God,
and unto Thee we ascribe glory:
to the Father, and to the Son,
and to the Holy Spirit,
now and ever and unto ages of ages.

Commentary: *This is the first of the "secret" prayers in the previous handbook. The new edition indicates that only those elements which make the progress of the Liturgy coherent are to be read aloud.*

The choir concludes the prayer with the "Amen" and begins singing the Trisagion. This song is called the hymn of the Holy Trinity. Following the examples of the angels, the earthly congregation dares to praise the Holy Trinity by singing:

Holy God! Holy Mighty! Holy Immortal!
Have mercy on us.
Holy God! Holy Mighty! Holy Immortal!
Have mercy on us.
Holy God! Holy Mighty! Holy Immortal!
Have mercy on us.

Glory to the Father, and to the Son,
and to the Holy Spirit, now and ever
and unto ages of ages. Amen.

Holy Immortal! Have mercy on us.
Holy God! Holy Mighty! Holy Immortal!
Have mercy on us.

After the Trisagion the priest says: "Peace be unto all!" The reader answers: "And to your spirit," and chants the prokeimenon.

The prokeimenon is a verse from a psalm and is sung as an introduction to the Epistle. The Epistle is most often taken from the letters of the apostles — letters they sent to the congregations which they had established. During the Easter season, the Epistle is taken from the Book of Acts.

After the reading of the Epistle the Alleluia ("Praise the Lord") is sung as a prelude to the Gospel, the Good News. The Alleluia, together with the censing done at the same time, indicates the holy presence of God.

Peace be unto all.

Just as the risen Christ greeted His disciples when He appeared to them, so the priest always says, "Peace be unto all" before reading the Gospel. While saying this, he blesses with his hand, his fingers forming the initials of Jesus Christ. The faithful bow their heads in acknowledgment.

With the proclamation of the Gospel, the encounter with the risen Lord, which began in the procession, continues. Because the Gospel is the teaching of the Lord Himself, all stand and listen with bowed heads.

Commentary: *Where the Liturgy is celebrated daily, the Gospels are read through almost entirely during the course of the year. Such opportunities to hear the Word are rare, so the faithful should read the daily gospel and epistle passages at home.*

The sermon follows the Gospel. Christ's promise, "When the Spirit of Truth come, He will guide you into all the truth" (Jn 16:13), is the basis for the sermon. The activity of this Spirit of Truth in the Liturgy means that the explanation of the Word is given in the name of the Church — it is not based on the preacher's own "excellence of speech" (I Cor 2:1).

Commentary: *Lists of names for intercessory prayers should be kept in the church. These may be titled "Lord save Thy servants" for the living, and "Give rest, O Lord, to the souls of Thy servants," for the dead.*

The Litany of Fervent Supplication follows the sermon. This litany is a responsory prayer in which the choir responds to each exhortation by singing "Lord have mercy" three times. The litany begins thus:

> Let us say with all our soul
> and with all our mind, let us say:
> O Lord almighty, the God of our fathers,
> we pray Thee, hearken and have mercy.
> Have mercy on us, O God,
> according to Thy goodness,
> we pray Thee, hearken and have mercy.

In contrast to the Great Litany, this litany contains prayers for individual members of the Church and their needs. The names of those, for instance, who are ill can be mentioned. Individuals may also request that deceased relatives be mentioned. Lits of names can be brought to church and given to the priest in the sanctuary. A Litany for the Departed is recited on those days designated as memorials for the dead and at funeral liturgies.

Commentary: *In certain circumstances, for example, when the Liturgy is broadcast on radio and time is short,* *it is possible to proceed from the Gospel and the sermon directly to the prayer "Again and oftentimes" and the Cherubic Hymn. The Greek Church has made a rule of this exception and omits all the litanies preceding the Cherubic Hymn.*

The Liturgy of the Word concludes with the Litany of the "Catechumens," or "Listeners," and the collect by the priest:

Let us, the faithful, pray for the catechumens,
that the Lord may have mercy on them.
That He will teach them the word of truth.
That He will reveal to them the gospel of
righteousness.
That He will unite them to His Holy, Catholic,
and Apostolic Church.

O Lord our God, who dwellest on high
and regardest the humble of heart; who hast
sent forth
as the salvation of the race of men
Thine only-begotten Son and God, our Lord
Jesus Christ;
Look down upon Thy servants the catechumens, who have bowed their necks before Thee;
make them worthy in due time of the laver
of regeneration,
the remission of sins, and the robe of incorrup-
tion. Unite them to Thy Holy, Catholic, and
Apostolic Church, and number them with Thy
chosen flock.
— That with us they may glorify
Thine all-honorable and majestic Name:
of the Father, and of the Son,

and of the Holy Spirit,
now and ever and unto ages of ages.

This litany prays for those who are to be joined to the Church through Baptism or who, as adults, are uniting themselves to the Orthodox Church in the sacrament of Chrismation, or Anointing.

These prayers remind us that the Church is not only for "us," but for God's work in the world. The words "Go into all the world and preach the gospel to the whole creation" (Mk 16:15) apply to us.

The Holy Gifts, the Bread and the Wine

THE GREAT ENTRANCE

In this part of the Liturgy the central event is also a procession, this time called the Great Entrance. Here the bread and wine prepared for Communion are taken from the side door of the sanctuary, carried down the side of the church to the front door, and from there up the center aisle to the solea and on through the Royal Doors to the Holy Table in the sanctuary.

Commentary: *At this point in the Liturgy, in the days before the present Proskomede existed, the deacons selected bread and wine for the thank offering from the gifts brought by the faithful. They then brought these into the Church and placed them on the Holy Table.*

In both processions in the Liturgy, the movement is towards the altar, which symbolizes the Kingdom of God. In this way the congregation is "lifted up" towards the Kingdom of God, where Christ, as Son of God, but also Son of Man, has already raised our human nature.

Commentary: *Alexander Schmemann writes of the eucharistic "lifting up":*

> *It is important to remember all this because, under the influence of the western understanding of the eucharist, we usually perceive the liturgy not in the key of ascent but of descent. The entire western eucharistic mystique is thoroughly imbued with the image of Christ descending onto our altars.*

Meanwhile, the original eucharistic experience, to which the very order of the eucharistic witnesses, speaks of our ascent to that place where Christ ascended, of the heavenly nature of the eucharistic celebration.

The eucharist is always a going out from "this world" and an ascent to heaven, and the altar is a symbol of the reality of this ascent, of its very "possibility." For Christ has ascended to heaven, and his altar is "sacred and spiritual." In "this world" there is not and cannot be *an altar, for the kingdom of God is "not of this world." And that is why it is so important to understand that we regard the altar with reverence — we kiss it, we bow before it, etc. — not because it is "sanctified" and has become, so to speak, a "sacred object," but because its very sanctification consists in its* referral *to the reality of the kingdom, in its conversion into a symbol of the kingdom. Our reverence and veneration is never related to "matter," but always to that which it reveals, of which it is an* epiphany, *i.e., a manifestation and presence* (The Eucharist. Sacrament of the Kingdom, SVS *Press 1988, pp. 60-1).*

The movement towards the altar is also a movement away from the world, for the Church as the Body of Christ is not of this world. But this withdrawal from the world takes place precisely for the sake of this same world. The withdrawal is always followed by a return to bear witness. The partaker of the Orthodox Eucharist bears witness with renewed strength to Christ who gave

Himself for the life of the whole world.

This part of the Liturgy contains what is known as the Litany of the Faithful, the Cherubic Hymn, during which the Great Entrance takes place, the prayer "for the precious gifts brought forth," the testimony of mutual love, and the Creed.

+

Let us, the faithful, again and again in peace pray to the Lord.

Again and oftentimes we fall down before Thee, O God who lovest mankind, that looking down upon our petition Thou wouldst cleanse our souls and bodies from all defilement of flesh and spirit; and grant us to stand blameless and without condemnation before Thy holy altar.

Grant also to those who pray with us, O God, growth in life and faith and spiritual understanding. Grant them to worship Thee blamelessly with fear and love, and to partake without condemnation of Thy Holy Mysteries, and to be accounted worthy of Thy heavenly Kingdom.

— That guarded always by Thy might we may ascribe glory unto Thee: to the Father, and to the Son, and to the Holy Spririt, now and ever and unto ages of ages.

After this Litany of the Faithful the priest reads a prayer which, in contrast to the other prayers in the

Liturgy, the priest offers on his own behalf in preparation for the thank offering. In the prayer, he asks for the power of the Holy Spirit to enable him to perform the sacrament, in which Christ Himself is both the Offerer and the Offered, the Receiver and the Received.

The words of this prayer express the important fact that in the Church the priesthood is Christ's priesthood. Christ, the only priest of the New Covenant, has made the Church a partaker both of His own priesthood and of the sacrifice offered for the life of the world.

Commentary: *If Christ Himself is both the Offerer of the congregation's sacrifice of thanks and the Sacrifice once-offered at Golgotha; if He is both the Receiver of the congregation's sacrifice of thanks and the One distributed in Holy Communion, what is the role of the priest when he asks for the power of the Holy Spirit in order to perform the service? It is this: the priest does not act as a substitute for Christ nor as Christ's representative, but his priesthood is Christ's priesthood, of which the Apostle says: ". . .this one, because he remains for ever, can never lose his priesthood" (Heb 7:24).*

Thus the mysteries of the Eucharist and the priesthood are linked together into one mystery, at the center of which is the "mystery of Christ." This is a great mystery, but I speak concerning Christ and the Church" (Eph 5:32).

After reading the prayer the priest incenses the altar, the icons of the Savior and the Mother of God, and the people. Meanwhile the singing of the Cherubic Hymn begins. It is sung slowly and with repetitions.

> Let us who mystically represent the
> Cherubim, and who sing the thrice-holy

> hymn to the life-creating Trinity, now
> lay aside all earthly care that we
> may receive the King of All, who
> comes invisibly upborne by the angelic
> hosts. Alleluia! Alleluia! Alleluia!

The Great Entrance takes place while the Cherubic Hymn is sung. In the sanctuary, the priest reads the Cherubic Hymn with hands uplifted, bows to the people asking for forgiveness (cf. Mt 5:23-24), and goes to the Table of Oblation. There he takes the bread and wine prepared for the sacrament and goes through the side door, carrying them out to where the people are. This procession, like the Little Entrance, goes down the side of the church to the church door, and from there up the middle to the solea, the altar platform. In this way the early custom of the people's bringing the elements for the holy sacrament as a thank offering comes out clearly. When he reaches the solea the priest prays:

> May the Lord God remember in His King-
> dom our most blessed Father the Bishop
> (name of the bishop of the diocese), all of
> you Orthodox Christians and all Christians
> always, now and ever and unto ages of
> ages.

Commentary: *In the Great Entrance the priest prays that the Lord God will remember the bishop of the diocese, and he goes on to say "and all of you Orthodox Christians and all Christians. . ." The word Orthodox means "right-believing" or also "rightly-praising" or "rightly-honoring." This is the attribute of the*

Eastern Church and its Christians in the same way that the Lutheran Church has the attribute Evangelical (Evangelical Lutheran) and that the Western Church is called Catholic (the Roman Catholic Church).

The term "right-believing Church," expresses the fact that our Church believes that through history it has preserved the original, evangelical (Gospel) teaching and tradition of the early and universal (catholic) Church. In the early Church the qualifying terms orthodox, catholic, and evangelical, were all in use at the same time for the same Church.

A person remembered by God is kept in His love and saving care. In His remembrance God makes no distinction between the living and the departed, for "all live to Him" (Lk 20:38).

Those who will receive Communion now step forward before the solea, and all the people bow their heads as the priest blesses them with the Holy Gifts.

Although the Holy Gifts have not yet been consecrated as the Body and Blood of Christ, they are already venerated, for in the Proskomede they were chosen and "foreseen" as the sacrifice of thanks to be offered.

The Great Entrance concludes as the priest, "clothed in the priesthood of Christ," raises the Holy Gifts, which are about to be brought to the altar as a sacrifice of thanks.

The final words of the Cherubic Hymn, "that we may receive the King of All, who comes invisibly upborne by the angelic hosts," are a reminder that the invisible heavenly host of saints also takes part in the Liturgy.

For the precious Gifts now offered,
let us pray to the Lord.

O Lord God almighty, who alone art holy,
who acceptest the sacrifice of praise
from those who call upon Thee with their
whole heart,
accept also the prayer of us sinners,
and bear it to Thy holy altar,
enabling us to offer unto Thee
gifts and spiritual sacrifices for our sins
and for the errors of the people.
Make us worthy to find grace in Thy sight,
that our sacrifice may be acceptable unto Thee,
and that the good spirit of Thy grace
may dwell upon us and upon these Gifts
here offered, and upon all Thy people.
— Through the compassions of Thine
only-begotten Son, with whom Thou are
blessed, together with Thine all-holy, good, and
life-creating Spirit,
now and ever and unto ages of ages.

After praying that the Spirit of God's grace come
upon the celebrants, the gifts, and all the people, the
priest greets the assembly:

Peace be with you all.

The deacon continues:

Let us love one another,
that with one mind we may confess.

In the early church, the faithful greeted one another
at this point with a "holy kiss," the men with the men,
the women with the women. Today, the priests ex-
change the kiss at the altar.

Commentary: *At this point in the Liturgy, following the custom of the Western Church, Orthodox church-goers could also greet one another, even with a hand-shake. Such a salutation of peace and love would express in a visible way the inner power of the faith of the community assembled together as the Body of Christ. It would confirm the awareness that "the love of God has been poured out in our hearts by the Holy Spirit who was given to us" (Rom 5:5).*

Father, Son, and Holy Spirit!
The Trinity, one in essence, and undivided!

The congregation responds indicating that faith in the Holy Trinity is to be confessed through love.

The deacon, standing on the solea, now says:

The doors! The doors!
In wisdom let us attend!

The words "The doors! The doors!" point to early Christian times, when the doorkeeper was asked to watch carefully to ensure that no one who was not a Christian should enter.

This is followed by the Creed, "I believe in one God." The Creed of Nicea-Constantinople was introduced into the order of the Liturgy in the sixth century; it had previously appeared in the baptismal celebration before the Liturgy.

The whole congregation sings the Creed:

I believe in one God, the Father almighty,
Maker of heaven and earth
and of all things visible and invisible.
And in one Lord Jesus Christ, the Son of God,
the only-begotten, begotten of the Father

before all ages. Light of Light;
true God of true God; begotten, not made;
of one essence with the Father,
by whom all things were made;
who for us men and for our salvation
came down from heaven, and was incarnate
of the Holy Spirit and the Virgin Mary,
and became man. And He was crucified for us
under Pontius Pilate, and suffered, and was
buried.
And the third day He rose again, according to
the Scriptures, and ascended into heaven,
and sits at the right hand of the Father;
and He shall come again with glory
to judge the living and the dead;
whose Kingdom shall have no end.
And in the Holy Spirit, the Lord,
the Giver of Life, who proceeds from the Father;
who with the Father and the Son together
is worshipped and glorified;
who spoke by the prophets.
And in one Holy, Catholic and Apostolic Church,
I acknowledge one baptism for the remission
of sins,
and the life of the world to come,
Amen.

The elevation of the Holy Gifts

THE ANAPHORA — SACRIFICE OF THANKS

We have reached the heart of the Liturgy, the Eucharist, "Eucharist" means "a sacrifice of thanks;" its prayers and actions are together called the "Anaphora," which in Greek means "offering."

The prayers of the Anaphora are comparable with New Testament texts, for the Eucharist was celebrated before the books of the New Testament existed. The Eucharist, in the form of a prayer of thanksgiving, expresses the teaching of the early Church about creation, the Fall, redemption and the unity of the heavenly and earthly congregation.

The Anaphora originated in the Passover meal which Christ had with His disciples before His Passion. It was there that He took bread, gave thanks, broke it and gave it to His disciples, saying: "'This is My body which is given for you.' And taking the cup of wine He said: 'This cup is the new covenant in my blood, which is shed for you'" (Lk 22:19-20; I Cor 11:23-25). Presenting His disciples with this model, Jesus instructed them: "Do this in remembrance of Me."

Commentary: *How the congregation's continuous verbal and bloodless thank offering to God corresponds to the sacrifice at Golgotha made just once for the life of the world is also a great mystery in the Eucharist. Here, in fact, the Apostle's exhortation is realized in practice: "Therefore by Him let us continually offer the sacrifice of praise to God, that is, the fruit of our lips, giving thanks to His Name" (Heb 13:15).*

We call this first Communion the "Communion of the Lord." In apostolic times, it was called the "breaking of bread."

After the outpouring of the Holy Spirit at Pentecost, the members of the first congregation began to celebrate Communion as the Lord had commanded them. We read that when the Apostle Paul went to Troas "on the first day of the week. . .the disciples came together to break bread" (Acts 20:7).

The prayer of thanksgiving, the breaking of bread, and the blessing of the cup have been an essential part of the Anaphora since the beginning (I Cor 10:16).

The Anaphora was very early understood as a thank offering, *eucharistia*. Around the year 100, the bishop and martyr Ignatius Theophorus urged the Ephesians: "Try to come together as often as possible to celebrate the eucharist of God and to praise Him."

In addition to the words of institution of Holy Communion and the offering of thanks, there is a third high point connected with the Anaphora. This is the "epiclesis," a prayer asking that the Holy Spirit be sent down upon the assembled congregation and upon the offered Gifts. John Chrysostom describes this prayer: at the Liturgy, the priest "stands before the altar with his hands raised to heaven calling upon the Holy Spirit to come down and touch the gifts thereon presented." (Nicon Patrinacos, *The Orthodox Liturgy* New Jersey, 1974, p. 323).

The Anaphora and the scriptural readings have formed the core of the Liturgy through the centuries. The other parts of the Liturgy have gradually grown around it.

+

> Let us stand aright! Let us stand with fear!
> Let us attend, that we may offer the Holy
> Oblation in peace.

With these words the deacon, standing outside the sanctuary, exhorts the people to prepare themselves for the holy sacrifice: the bringing of the Holy Gifts, the bread and wine, as a verbal thank offering to God.

> A mercy of peace! A sacrifice of praise!

Thus the people respond, saying that they are ready to bring the thank offering to God as an offering of peace and mercy.

> The grace of our Lord Jesus Christ,
> the love of God the Father,
> and the communion of the Holy Spirit
> be with you all.

With this apostolic salutations (2 Cor 13:14), the priest summons three sources of power to help the faithful: the grace of the Lord Jesus, the love of God the Father and the communion of the Holy Spirit.

> And with you spirit.

The priest needs the same power in order to perform the holy sacrifice.

> Let us lift up our hearts,
> We lift them up unto the Lord.

With this liturgical exhortation, which is even older than the apostolic salutation, the priest wants to confirm, as it were, that the congregation is in fact ready to fulfill the next request:

Let us give thanks unto the Lord.
It is meet and right.

Having heard the people's response, the priest begins the eucharistic prayer of thanksgiving. In this
prayer man, who represents all creation, is in the
position in which God placed him at the beginning.
Man alone is capable of giving thanks for his existence
and for the other gifts of the Creator. He is the only
"eucharistic" being in creation.

And man, awakened from the Fall, experiences the
closeness of the Kingdom of God again and again — as
in the present service, which God receives.

It is meet and right to hymn Thee, to bless
Thee, to praise Thee, to give thanks to Thee,
and to worship Thee in every place of Thy
dominion: for Thou art God ineffable, incon-
ceivable, invisible, incomprehensible, ever-
existing and eternally the same, Thou and
Thine only-begotten Son and Thy Holy
Spirit. Thou it was who brought us from
non-existence into being, and when we had
fallen away didst raise us up again, and didst
not cease to do all things until Thou hadst
brought us up to heaven and hadst endowed
us with Thy Kingdom which is to come. For
all these things we give thanks to Thee and
to Thine only-begotten Son, and to Thy
Holy Spirit; for all things of which we know
and of which we know not, whether mani-
fest or unseen; and we thank Thee for this
Liturgy which Thou hast found worthy to

accept at our hands, though there stand by
Thee thousands of archangels and hosts of
angels, the Cerubim and the Seraphim, six-
winged, many-eyed, who soar aloft, borne
on their pinions, singing the triumphant
hymn, shouting, proclaiming and saying:

Holy! Holy! Holy! Lord of Sabaoth!
Heaven and earth are full of Thy glory!
Hosanna in the highest!
Blessed is He that comes in the Name of the
Lord!
Hosanna in the highest!

As in the prophet Isaiah's vision (Is 6:1-3), God's
praying people are lifted up before the throne of God.
"Heaven and earth," angels and people, join in the same
triumphal song and greet the eucharistic Christ: "Hosanna," which means: "Help! Save!"

With these blessed powers,
O Master who lovest mankind,
we also cry aloud and say:
Holy art Thou, and all-holy,
Thou and Thine only-begotten Son
and Thy Holy Spirit!
Holy art Thou and all-holy
and magnificent is Thy glory!
Who hast so loved thy world
as to give Thine only-begotten Son,
that whoever believes in Him
should not perish but have everlasting life;
who when He had come and had fulfilled

all the dispensation for us,
in the night in which He was given up
— or rather, gave Himself up for the life of
the world —
took bread in His holy, pure, and blameless
hands;
and when He had given thanks and blessed it,
and hallowed it, and broken it,
He gave it to His holy disciples and apostles,
saying: "Take! Eat! This is My Body
which is broken for you,
for the remission of sins."
And likewise, after supper, He took the cup,
saying: "Drink of it, all of you!
This is My Blood of the New Testament,
which is shed for you and for many
for the remission of sins!"

The love of God the Father was revealed in His Son,
who was "obedient to the point of death" (Phil 2:8),
and who, in His perfect love, "Himself bore our sins in
His own pure and unblemished sacrifice for our sins
and instituted the sacrament that takes place by the
power of the Holy Spirit, saying: 'As often as you do
this, do it in remembrance of me'" (Prayer of Ambrose
of Milan).

All this commemoration is the proclamation again
and again of the Death and Resurrection of Christ (1
Cor 11:26), the experience of all that happened in the
past as real and present at this moment.

The priest raises the Holy Gifts, the bread and
wine, crossing his hands, and says:

> Thine own of Thine own
> we offer unto Thee,
> on behalf of all and for all.

As a result of all that has happened, the bread and wine, symbolizing Christ's body and blood — God's own gifts chosen from His own gifts — are now offered or sacrificed *for* all. This is what God grants through the sacrifice at Golgotha.

Commentary: *The words "on behalf of all and for all" are explained in different ways, even by Greek interpreters. The author regards the explanation given here as the one most applicable to the Eucharist as a whole.*

After these words, the whole congregation joins in the verbal offering and sings:

> We praise Thee, we bless Thee,
> we give thanks unto Thee, O Lord,
> and we pray to Thee, O our God.

Commentary: *When the Anaphora is read aloud in the hearing of the congregation, the music for the responses of the congregation should be correspondingly brief.*

The sung portions of the Anaphora, often called "A Mercy of peace," generally date from the time when the prayers were read "secretly." Thus rather long compositions were needed to take up the time it took to read the prayers. But in the present circumstance, where the Anaphora is read aloud, the use of these often concert-like compositions is unsuitable and interferes with the whole.

The epiclesis prayer is a direct continuation of the song. In this prayer the priest, acting as the mouthpiece of the whole people of God, raises his hands (1 Tim 2:8) and prays that the Holy Spirit be sent down upon the congregation and the Holy Gifts.

Commentary: *The mystery is also in the fact that, although the priest, "clothed in the priesthood of Christ," offers the eucharistic sacrifice to God in the manner described above, he is acting not only for the congregation present but also with them, thus forming the fulness of the Church. The people of God, the "fruit of whose lips" the priest sets forth as a sacrifice of praise, are just as essential for the Eucharist as the priest.*

Apart from the one prayer already mentioned which the priest reads expressly on his own behalf, all the prayers of the Liturgy are in the plural, as for example "we offer unto Thee" or "we. . .ask Thee, and pray Thee and supplicate Thee: Send down Thy Holy Spirit upon us and upon these Gifts here offered."

This type of common prayer requires that the assembled congregation, the people of God, hear what they are asking, praying, and supplicating, as well as what they hope and believe they will receive: "Send down Thy Holy Spirit upon us and upon these Gifts here offered."

The fact that rubrics in the handbook indicate that the Eucharistic prayers are to be read "secretly" is regarded as an obstacle to reading them aloud, and is interpreted to mean that the priest is to read prayers to himself.

Metropolitan Emilianos of Silibria has studied the manuscripts of the Liturgy in libraries of Athens, Grottaferrata, and Leningrad and discovered that the term "secret prayers" did not appear in texts of the Liturgy until after the thirteenth century. In 1959, Emilianos, then still an archimandrite, published two works about the participation of the people in the Liturgy: To "Amen" en te Theia Leitourgia *(The "Amen" in the Divine Liturgy)* and He Leitourgia mas *(Our Liturgy).* In these writings the author asks: *"How can the people say amen (it is truly so), if they have not heard what has just been said? How can the* ekphonesis *(the final words, to be said aloud) be spoken if all have not heard the prayer that preceded it?"*

As early as 1932, there was an excellent article on the same subject in the theological periodical Living Tradition *(in Russian, YMCA Press; Finnish translation in* Ortodoksia 34, Kuopio 1984) by the Finnish Dr. Boris Sove, entitled "The Eucharist in the early Church and present practice."

In this connection another work that deserves mention is The Orthodox Liturgy *(New Jersey, 1974) by the American priest and theologian Dr. Nicon Patrinacos. One part of the book is a survey of the development of the Orthodox Liturgy from the second century to the present. In this work dedicated to the Orthodox congregations of America, with a foreword by Archbishop Iakovos, the author criticizes the custom of reading the prayers of the Liturgy "secretly," regarding it as a Byzantine relic. He points to the 137th Novella of Emperor Justinian (565 A.D.) which required priests, under threat of punishment, to read the eucharistic and baptismal prayers in a voice loud enough for the people to hear (p. 310). Patrinacos is of the opinion that, because the Liturgy has developed continuously, as is evident in history, its development cannot now be* stopped for "*the need for reforming our liturgy is not only obvious but urgent*" (p. 315).

Lastly, another American theologian, Alexander Schmemann, in a book already cited, speaks of three unsatisfactory points in liturgical practice (ibid, pp. 304-306).

The first item he mentions is an excessive symbolism which attaches an allegorical meaning to every point in the Liturgy, so that many details are interpreted "*as what they are not.*"

His second point is about the secret prayers in the Liturgy. He writes:

> The second defect consists of the secret prayers, *as a result of which the overwhelming majority of the laity do not know and never even hear the text of the eucharist itself and are thus deprived of this priceless treasure. No one has ever explained why the* "*chosen race, a royal priesthood, holy nation, God's own people, that they may declare the wonderful deeds of him who called them out of darkness*" *(1 Pet 12:9) cannot listen to the prayers that they offer to God.*
>
> The third defect is the distinction between the clergy and the laity during communion, distinction with tragic consequences for church consciousness. . .
>
> Defects of this sort can add up to a great multitude, but this subject remains a kind of incomprehensible taboo, and neither the hierarchy nor the theologians seem to take notice of it. This needs to be done, but no one is permitted to discuss the matter. Yet

> *I repeat what I have repeated many times*
> *already in this book: what concerns the*
> *eucharist concerns the Church, and what*
> *concerns the Church concerns the eucharist,*
> *so that any ailment in the liturgy reflects on*
> *our faith and on the whole life of the Church.*

It should be said, with regard to Schmemann's and the other theologians' well-founded criticisms, that nowadays in more and more Orthodox churches — particularly in the West, where services are celebrated in the language of the people, but also in many places in Greece — the eucharistic prayers are read aloud in the hearing of the people.

In the Finnish Orthodox Church, the second and third shortcomings mentioned by Schmemann have been eliminated in the 1985 handbook. The prayers of the Liturgy are to be read aloud and the clergy are not to be separated behind closed doors from the rest of the people of God during Communion. The prayer before Communion is to be recited together, and Communion is to be given to the faithful immediately after it is given to the clergy.

> Again we offer unto Thee
> this reasonable and bloodless worship,
> and ask Thee, and pray Thee,
> and supplicate Thee:
> Send down Thy Holy Spirit upon us
> and upon these Gifts here offered.

After this prayer the priest blesses first the Bread, then the Cup, and then both together, saying:

And make this Bread the precious Body of
Thy Christ. Amen.
And that which is in the Cup,
the precious Blood of Thy Christ. Amen.
Making the change by Thy Holy Spirit.
Amen. Amen. Amen.

After hearing these words of blessing over the
Bread and Wine, the congregation, in unison with the
priest, says:

Amen. Amen. Amen.

Commentary: *The mystery is also the Communion
itself, which is called the "Holy Mystery." Orthodox
tradition has not attempted to explain in a scholastic
fashion just how the bread and wine change to the
elements of communion. As the Liturgy itself describes
it, the Holy Gifts, the bread and the wine, simply
become the true Body and precious Blood of Christ
through the operation of the Holy Spirit, without being
changed in their appearance. They are Holy Communion regardless of the sense in which we receive
them. A person who partakes of Communion in faith
receives it "for the remission of his sins and unto life
everlasting." The following words apply to anyone
who receives Communion without faith: "He who eats
and drinks in an unworthy manner eats and drinks
judgment to himself, not discerning the Lord's Body"
(1 Cor 11:29).*

As they join in the priest's amen, the people bow to
the ground before Christ in the Holy Gifts.

Commentary: *According to the rules of the Church,
bowing to the ground is not done on Sundays and feast*

days. However, because parish services are for the most part held only those days, in practice the rule is not followed to the letter, and such bows are made even on Sundays.

In Greek monasteries and elsewhere, according to local customs, it is also possible to kneel during the holiest moment of the Liturgy, from the beginning of the hymn "We praise Thee" to the Amen.

A clear rule forbids bowing to the ground between Easter and Pentecost. But on the day of Pentecost there are prayers during which the whole congregation kneels, as is even written into the order of the service.

In the Lenten Liturgy and other services in Lent prostrations by the clergy and congregation are a typical feature of the services. Bowing to the ground, and rising to one's feet immediately, symbolize the Fall of man and his rising from it through repentance. A person who has been to Communion does not prostrate himself on the same day, for partaking of Communion is his Passover.

The prayer of the epiclesis asks further that the Holy Spirit should descend not only upon the communion Gifts but also upon the faithful. This is in order that the Holy Spirit may influence the minds and hearts of the faithful, that as they receive Holy Communion they may feel Christ to be their own life (Col 3:4).

This, now, is the first prayer after the blessing of the Gifts:

> That they may be to those who partake
> for the purification of soul,
> for the remission of sins,
> for the communion of Thy Holy Spirit,

for the fulfillment of the Kingdom of Heaven,
for boldness towards Thee,
and not for judgment or condemnation.

The prayer continues as a eucharistic remembrance.
The eucharistic Christ is not alone; He is with His whole
Church, His whole Body. He gathers together "in one all
things in Christ, both which are in heaven and which are
on earth" (Eph 1:10). The first to be remembered are
those who are "in heaven," the souls of the saints who
have died in the faith, so that the Eucharist may be a
consolation to them, that they "may rejoice gladdened
in praise and holy glory" (Ambrose of Milan).

Again we offer unto Thee this reasonable
worship for those who have fallen asleep in
the faith: ancestors, fathers, patriarchs,
prophets, apostles, preachers, evangelists,
martyrs, confessors, ascetics, and every
righteous spirit made perfect in faith.

Especially for our most holy, most pure,
most blessed and glorious Lady,
Theotokos and ever-virgin Mary.

The holy Virgin Mary has a special place among the
saints. Her willing consent — "Behold the maidservant
of the Lord! Let it be to me according to Thy word"
—was just as necessary as the influence of the Spirit of
God: "The Holy Spirit will come upon you, and the
power of the Highest will overshadow you."

By her consent, she, as the representative of the
whole of mankind, "found favor with God" to serve
the "mystery of salvation" and remained ever-virgin.
As the Mother of God, who gave "bodily form" to the

Son of God, she is a symbol of the Church, the mystical Body of Christ.

All generations will call her blessed (Lk 1:48). This happens in the Liturgy too as the people sing:

> It is truly meet to bless you, O Theotokos,
> ever-blessed and most pure,
> and the Mother or our God.
> More honorable than the Cherubim,
> and more glorious beyond compare than the Seraphim:
> without defilement you gave birth to God the Word:
> true Theotokos, we magnify you.

Commentary: *At this point in the Liturgy, on the great feast and certain days, the ninth irmos of the canon with its refrains is sung instead of the hymn "It is truly meet." The canon is a group of nine songs from Matins, and the first stanza of each song is called an "irmos."*

The ninth irmos of the canon for the Easter period is "Shine, Shine! O new Jerusalem," and it is preceded by the refrain "The angel cried to the Lady full of grace."

The Church, however, prays not only for the saints glorified by God, but also for the whole world and all mankind. The world too is the object of God's love, and Christ was crucified and rose for the life of the whole world. But the world is overpowered by evil and "the whole creation groans and labors with birth pangs together until now" (Rom 8:22). The world is called to turn from pride, selfishness and self-sufficiency, for otherwise it has no part in the Kingdom of God, which

is "righteousness and peace and joy in the Holy Spirit"
(Rom 14:17).

The priest continues the eucharistic prayer:

> Again we offer unto Thee this reasonable
> worship: for the whole world;
> for the Holy, Catholic, and Apostolic Church;
> for those who live in chastity and holiness;
> for all civil authorities;
> grant them, O Lord, peaceful times,
> that we, in their tranquility,
> may lead a calm and peaceful life
> in all godliness and sanctity.

The priest goes on to ask that the Lord remember
the bishop of the diocese and the faithful where they
dwell and all those who need God's special care, such
as the sick, the oppressed, those persecuted for their
faith. Gifts of mercy for all are asked of God, so that

> with one mouth and one heart
> we may praise Thine all-honorable
> and majestic Name: of the Father
> and of the Son, and of the Holy Spirit,
> now and ever and unto ages of ages.

The Anaphora ends with the priest's blessing:

> And the mercies of our great God
> and Savior Jesus Christ
> shall be with all of you.

With these words the priest expresses the desire that
the faithful who are present may also receive the gifts of
mercy which were asked for those different tasks and
situations.

Communion

COMMUNION

The next part of the Liturgy is the beginning of preparation for Holy Communion. The faithful pray that God may make them worthy of partaking of the Holy Gifts.

Just before Communion is given, the priest raises the Holy Bread, urges the people to pay attention, and says: "The holy things for the holy," that is, the Holy Gifts are only for holy people. A similar exhortation is to be found as early as the first century in the description of the thanksgiving meal: "If anyone is holy, let him advance; if anyone is not, let him be converted." (*Didache* 10:6). A similar theme of repentance appears in the apostle's exhortation: "Let a man examine himself, and so let him eat of that bread and drink of that cup" (1 Cor 11:28).

In what sense is the word "holy" used here? This is made clear in the prayers in this part of the Liturgy.

+

The Eucharist, the sacrifice of thanks, has already been offered — transferred, as it were, to God's heavenly altar of sacrifice. In this new situation, mercy and the gift of the Holy Spirit are invoked on the congregation now present:

> Having remembered all the saints,
> again and again in peace let us pray to the Lord.
> For the precious Gifts offered and sanctified,

let us pray to the Lord.
That our God, who loves mankind,
receiving them upon His holy, heavenly,
and ideal altar as a sweet spiritual fragrance,
will send down upon us in return
His divine grace and the gift of the Holy Spirit,
let us pray to the Lord.
For our deliverance from all affliction, wrath,
danger and necessity, let us pray to the Lord.
Help us, save us, have mercy on us,
and keep us, O God, by Thy grace.

The choir responds by singing "Lord, have mercy" after each sentence. In the following litany, they respond "Grant it, O Lord."

The litany of supplication is each person's examination of the state of his own soul, asking for forgiveness and for everything necessary in order to live his life to the end in unity of the faith and the communion of the Holy Spirit.

That the whole day may be perfect, holy,
peaceful and sinless, let us ask of the Lord.
An angel of peace, a faithful guide, a guardian
of our souls and bodies, let us ask of the Lord.
Pardon and remission of our sins and transgressions, let us ask of the Lord.
All things that are good and profitable for our
souls, and peace for the world,
let us ask of the Lord.
A Christian ending to our life: painless, blameless,
and peaceful; and a good defense before the
dread judgment seat of Christ,
let us ask of the Lord.

> Having asked for the unity of the Faith,
> and the communion of the Holy Spirit,
> let us commend ourselves and each other,
> and all our life unto Christ our God.

The next prayer shows us that Holy Communion is received for the "remission of sins" and "forgiveness of transgressions." Thus we go to Communion not perfect and sinless, but precisely because we are sinful and imperfect. But we pray that God will make us worthy of partaking of the holy meal "with a pure conscience." Even though only God can make us sinners worthy, it remains our task to see that our conscience is pure when we partake of the Holy Gifts. And it can be pure only when we feel sincere repentance and a desire to do better.

The Lord's Prayer, which the people sing, likewise reminds us of what is needed for a pure conscience: we cannot expect forgiveness from God if we ourselves have not forgiven everyone. Only when we have granted forgiveness can we, "with boldness and without condemnation," approach our heavenly Father.

> Unto Thee we commend our whole life and
> our hope, O Master who lovest mankind.
> We ask Thee, and pray Thee, and supplicate
> Thee:
> make us worthy to partake of the heavenly
> and awesome Mysteries of this sacred and
> spiritual table with a pure conscience: for
> remission of sins,
> for forgiveness of transgressions,
> for the communion of the Holy Spirit,
> for the inheritance of the Kingdom of Heaven,

for boldness towards Thee,
but not for judgment or condemnation.
— And make us worthy, O Master, that with
boldness and without condemnation we may
dare to call on Thee, the heavenly God, as
Father, and to say:

Our Father who art in heaven,
hallowed by Thy name.
Thy Kingdom come.
Thy will be done, on earth as it is in heaven.
Give us this day our daily bread;
and forgive us our trespasses,
as we forgive those who trespass against us;
and lead us not into temptation,
but deliver us from evil.

Commentary: *A prostration is made on weekdays
at the beginning of the Lord's Prayer.*

After the people have sung the Lord's Prayer and the
priest has completed it with words of praise, he wishes
peace to all and asks them to bow to the Lord.

. . .Look down from heaven, O Master,
upon those who have bowed their heads
unto Thee, the awesome God.
Do Thou Thyself, O Master, distribute these
gifts here offered, unto all of us for good,
according to the individual need of each. . .
— Through the grace and compassion and
love toward mankind of Thine only-
begotten Son, with whom Thou art blessed,
together with Thine all-holy, good, and
life-creating Spirit, now and ever, and
unto ages of ages.

After praying with bowed head on behalf of the people, that each should receive, by the grace, mercy, and compassion of the Son of God, those gifts which are of benefit to that individual, the priest continues the prayer, turning now to the invisibly present Christ. He prays that Christ by His "mighty hand," that is His divine power, should bless both those who distribute and those who receive Communion.

Attend, O Lord Jesus Christ our God,
out of Thy holy dwelling-place,
from the throne of glory of Thy Kingdom;
and come sanctify us, O Thou who sittest on
high with the Father,
and art here invisibly present with us;
and by Thy mighty hand
impart to us Thy most pure Body
and precious Blood,
and through us to all the people.

Having prayed that Christ should bless the people present with His holiness, the priest elevates the Holy Communion Bread and says:

The Holy Things for the holy!

Commentary: *In the fourteenth-century commentaries of the Church Fathers we read: "After the Lamb has been shown to the people the priest says: 'The Holy Things for the holy!'" This statement reflects a time when the altar was arranged in such a way that the priest stood behind it, facing the people.*

The congregation responds by declaring in song that holiness is Christ's only:

One is Holy. One is the Lord Jesus Christ,
to the glory of God the Father. Amen.

The Breaking of Bread, already known in the New
Testament, follows. Just one bread is broken, recalling
the words of the Apostle: "Because there is one loaf, we
who are many are one body, for we all partake of the
same loaf" (1 Cor 10:17). As he breaks the Communion
Bread, which is called the Lamb, the priest says:

Divided and distributed is the Lamb of God:
who is divided, yet not disunited;
who is ever eaten, yet never consumed,
but sanctifying those who partake thereof.

After these words, the "communion verse" and
verses from Psalm 34 are sung.

Then, after the Communion Bread has been broken
into four parts, the priest takes the portion inscribed
with the letters "IC" and puts it into the chalice, saying:
"The fullness of the Holy Spirit."

After blessing a cup of hot water with the words:
"Blessed is the warmth of Thy Holy Things," the priest
pours a sufficient quantity of "warmth" into the chalice.

Next the priest takes the part of the Lamb inscribed
with the letters "XC" and divides it into as many parts
as needed for the priests and deacons who will com-
mune. He divides the remaining two portions into
sufficient pieces for all the people.

Having done all this, the priest, together with his
concelebrants, bows to the ground and prays for God's
forgiveness. Then he rises, bows to his concelebrants,
and asks their forgiveness. Finally, he bows also to the

people, comes to the solea, and bids those who have prepared themselves for Communion to draw near:

In the fear of God, and with faith, draw near!

Commentary: *If the bishop is present but not himself celebrating the Liturgy, when Communion is ready to be distributed, he comes, faces the people, and says: "In the fear of God, and with faith, draw near." Then he kneels before the altar and recites the prayer: "I believe, O Lord, and I confess."*

The people sing:

Blessed is He that comes in the Name of the Lord!
God is the Lord and has revealed Himself to us!

Commentary: *We know that, from the earliest history of the church, the whole Liturgy was kept as a holy secret which no outsider was permitted to watch. Not even the learners who were being prepared for Holy Baptism and the Anointing of the Holy Spirit could be present at the Liturgy of the Faithful, when the Holy Eucharist was being celebrated. The faithful who remained, specifically as members of the Church, took part in Communion, the holy Love Feast of perfect unity, in faith. In those days everyone present participated in Communion.*

When the number of Christians multiplied after the period of the martyrs ended, the original principle concerning presence at the Liturgy was no longer followed in practice. Even John Chrysostom in his sermons reprimanded those who did not stay to the end of the Liturgy. The same situation continues to this day. At the Liturgy there may be people present who, for one reason or another, do not take part in Communion. Among them may also be some who are not members of the Orthodox Church. As stated at the beginning of this book, receiving Communion is the only thing that those who do not belong to the Church may not do. This is by no means because they are considered to be worse Christians than the Orthodox. The latter take part in Communion precisely because of their inferiority, and they confess at the same time that they are the greatest sinners. Thus the personality of the non-Orthodox person is not an issue but rather the fact that everything must take place in accordance with the biblical words: "Let all things be done decently and in order" (1 Cor 14:40). Holy Baptism and Chrismation precede Communion. A person who has already been baptized in the Name of the Triune God — Father, Son and Holy Spirit — is not baptized a second time. The sacrament of the Anointing of the Holy Spirit is thus the door to membership in the Church. And everyone who is a member of the people of God has permission to take part both in the prayers of the Liturgy and in Communion. This order is also followed because, although going to Communion does require a decision on the part of each individual, it is not primarily an expression of personal piety nor of satisfying spiritual needs; rather, it is the common ascent of all the people of God towards the Love Feast of the Kingdom of God and the experience of holy togetherness and unity in it.

Those who are to receive Communion now step forward before the solea and, following the priest's example, kneel and in unison say this prayer, which each one should memorize:

> I believe, O Lord, and I confess
> that Thou art truly the Christ,
> the Son of the living God,
> who camest into the world to save sinners,
> of whom I am first. I believe also
> that this is truly Thine own most pure Body,
> and that this is truly Thine own precious
> Blood.
>
> Therefore, I pray Thee: Have mercy upon
> me and forgive my transgressions
> both voluntary and involuntary, of word and
> of deed, committed in knowledge or in
> ignorance.
>
> And make me worthy to partake without
> condemnation of Thy most pure Mysteries,
> for the remission of my sins,
> and unto life everlasting.
>
> Of Thy Mystical Supper, O Son of God,
> accept me today as a communicant;
> for I will not speak of Thy Mystery to Thine
> enemies, neither like Judas will I give Thee a
> kiss;
> but like a thief will I confess Thee;
> Remember me, O Lord, in Thy Kingdom.
>
> May the communion of Thy holy Mysteries
> be neither to my judgment, nor to my
> condemnation, O Lord, but to the healing of
> soul and body.

Commentary: *According to the custom of the Greek church the prayer "I believe, O Lord and I confess. . ." is not read to the people separately after the priest's communion. Rather the priest reads it aloud on his knees before the holy altar. In this way the people may also see the holy gifts on the altar, which the priest may motion towards during the words "This is your pure body and this is your precious blood."*

After the prayer is finished, all bow to the ground, following the priest's example. They bow before Christ Himself, whose pure Body and precious Blood are on the Altar Table.

The priests and deacons now receive Communion at the altar. Meanwhile, the choir repeats the prayer just said, singing "Of Thy Mystical Supper, O Son of God. . . ."

Commentary: *Priests and deacons receive holy communion first, from the side of the altar table. The identity of the clergy with the people of God is not broken for immediately all recite together: "Of thy mystical supper. . ." The clergy receive the bread first, then the wine. In the liturgy of the Apostle James the faithful also receive communion in this way: The priest offers the communion bread and the deacon offers the chalice.*

When the clergy have received Communion the priest and deacon come to the Royal Doors to give Communion to the people. At the same time the choir begins to sing:

> Receive the Body of Christ;
> taste the fountain of immortality.
> Alleluia! Alleleuia! Alleluia!

The faithful approach in one or more lines, depending on how many chalices are offered. Reaching the cup, each person in turn crosses his arms on his breast and audibly says his first name. This enables the priest to add the communicant's name to the words: "The servant (handmaiden) of God (name), partakes of the precious and holy Body and Blood of our Lord and God and Savior Jesus Christ, for the remission of sins and unto life everlasting." The communicant opens his mouth, and the priest gives him Holy Communion with the communion spoon.

After receiving Communion, each person kisses the chalice as if it were the Savior's side from which blood and water flowed.

It should be mentioned that the sign of the Cross is not made in front of the chalice, but only after one has stepped aside.

After receiving Communion, the individual goes to the place where a piece of church bread and some water sweetened with wine are offered. This custom, originally a monastic practice, is a reminder of the agape or love feast of the early Church, which was joined to the Communion service.

Those who have received Communion do not go back to their places immediately but bow their heads and receive the priest's blessing:

> O God, save Thy people,
> and bless Thine inheritance.

And they listen to a hymn about the Light which has come to them:

> We have seen the true light!
> We have received the heavenly Spirit!
> We have found the true Faith!
> Worshipping the undivided Trinity,
> who has saved us.

Finally, the priest turns to the people and blesses them with the communion cup, saying:

> Blessed is our God,
> always, now and ever
> and unto ages of ages.

This final bringing forth of the communion cup is interpreted symbolically to mean Christ's Ascension to heaven. The faithful bow before the Communion Gifts and go back to their places as the apostles went from the Mount of Olives: "And they worshipped Him and returned to Jerusalem with great joy" (Lk 24:50-52).

The final bowing before the Holy Cup

THANKSGIVING FOR COMMUNION

After receiving Communion, the congregation con-
centrates on thanking God for the Holy Gifts received.
The priest in the sanctuary reads Easter hymns to
himself: "Behold through the Cross joy has come into
all the world." In the Eucharist too one passes through
the Cross to the Resurrection. The fulfillment of this is
an experience of the joy of Easter: the risen Lord
offers a feast of the Kingdom of God.

+

Let our mouths be filled with Thy praise,
O Lord, that we may sing of Thy glory;
for Thou hast made us worthy to partake
of Thy holy, divine, immortal,
and life-creating Mysteries.

To partake of the divine Mysteries is to become a
partaker of Christ Himself, of His "divine nature" (2
Pet 1:4). The Apostle Paul characterizes his experience
of this relationship as follows: "It is no longer I who
live, but Christ lives in me; and the life which I now
live in the flesh I live by faith in the Son of God, who
loved me and gave Himself for me" (Gal 2:20).

Thus in the hymn of thanks which follows there is
the further prayer that this holy relationship to Christ
may be preserved in us as long as we "live in the
flesh," to the end of this life, and that we may live

according to Christ's truth and witness to it as did the
holy martyrs.

> Keep us in Thy holiness
> that all the day we may meditate upon Thy
> righteousness.
> Alleluia! Alleluia! Alleluia!

A litany of thanksgiving follows:

> Let us attend! Having partaken of the
> divine, holy, most pure, immortal,
> heavenly, life-creating, and awesome
> Mysteries of Christ,
> let us worthily give thanks unto the Lord.
> Help us, save us, have mercy on us.
> and keep us, O God, by Thy grace.
> Asking that the whole day may be
> perfect, holy, peaceful and sinless,
> let us commend ourselves and each other,
> and all our life unto Christ our God.

The litany of thanksgiving concludes with a prayer
in which we ask God to strengthen us to walk on the
right path according to His commandments, through
the intercessions of the Mother of God and all the
saints.

> We thank Thee, O Master who lovest mankind,
> Benefactor of our souls,
> that Thou hast made us worthy this day
> of Thy heavenly and immortal mysteries.
> Make straight our path;
> strengthen us all in Thy fear;
> guard our life; make firm our steps;
> through the prayers and supplications

of the glorious Theotokos
and ever-virgin Mary
and of all Thy saints.

This thanksgiving part of the Liturgy recalls the ending of the first Communion. Matthew wrote: "And when they had sung a hymn they went out to the Mount of Olives" (Mt 26:30).

The Liturgy has ended

THE ENDING OF THE LITURGY

The Eucharist has been completed. The Communion Gifts are no longer on the Holy Table. The celebrating priest also goes out of the altar into the midst of the people to read the final prayers of the Liturgy and to give the final blessing.

+

Let us depart in peace.

These words, with which the priest prepares the people to depart, can also be interpreted to mean our taking Christ's peace from the Liturgy out into the world.

The people respond that they leave "in the Name of the Lord."

Asking the people to join in prayer — "Let us pray to the Lord" — the priest goes to the middle of the church to read the prayer which is appropriately called the "Prayer before the Ambo" (the ambo is the platform in the center of the church).

O Lord, who blessest those who bless Thee,
and sanctifiest those who trust in Thee:
save Thy people and bless Thine inheritance.
Preserve the fullness of Thy Church.
Sanctify those who love the beauty of Thy house;
and forsake us not who put our hope in Thee.

Give peace to Thy world, to Thy churches,
to Thy priests, to all those in civil authority,
to all Thy people.
For every good gift and every perfect gift
is from above, coming down from Thee,
the Father of Lights,
and unto Thee we ascribe glory, thanksgiving, and worship:
to the Father, and to the Son, and to the
Holy Spirit,
now and ever and unto ages of ages.

God is the Father of Lights, or the Father of the Son
and the Holy Spirit. All that we receive in the Liturgy is
God's perfect gift, including even the holiness of Christ
who alone is holy, which He gives us as a gift of love.

Three times the choir sings:

Blessed be the Name of the Lord
henceforth and forevermore.

Praising the Name of the Lord introduces the Lord's
blessing, which the priest now proclaims:

The blessing of the Lord be upon you
through His grace and love for mankind
always, now and ever and unto ages of ages.

As he pronounces the blessing, the priest, as the
bearer of Christ's priesthood, raises his right hand and
blesses the people with the sign of the Cross. The
model for this is Christ's Ascension: "And He led them
as far as Bethany, and He lifted up His hands and
blessed them" (Lk 24:50).

> Glory to Thee, O Christ
> our God and our hope,
> glory to Thee!

The singers conclude this exclamation of the priest, giving glory "to the Father, and to the Son, and to the Holy Spirit, now and ever and unto ages of ages." The words referring to time, "now and ever and unto ages of ages," so often repeated in Orthodox worship, have their own message. Only the present moment is available for our use at any given time, but this moment contains the past and the future. In the Eucharist, the past is lived as present and the future is already present. The same happens in the soul of the Christian: "The narrow way has no end: its quality is eternity."

Commentary: *The citation in full is as follows:*

The narrow way has no end: its quality is eternity. There every moment is a moment of beginning—the present includes the future: the day of judgment; the present includes the past: creation; for Christ is timelessly present everywhere, both in hell and in heaven. With the coming of the One, plurality disappears, even in time and space. Everything happens simultaneously, now and here and everywhere, in the depth of your heart. There you meet what you sought: the depth and height and breadth of the Cross: the Saviour and salvation.

Therefore, if you wish to save your soul and win eternal life, arise moment by moment from your fullness, bless yourself

> *with the sign of the Cross and say: Let me,*
> *Lord, make a good beginning, in the*
> *name of the Father and of the Son and of*
> *the Holy Ghost. Amen.*
> (Tito Colliander, *Way of the Ascetics*, Crest-
> wood; St Vladimir's Seminary Press, 1985,
> pp. 100-1).

The prayer "Lord have mercy" is added once more
to the doxology, and then the priest is asked: "Father,
bless."

The priest gives the final blessing:

> May Christ, our true God,
> through the prayers of His most pure Mother,
> of the Holy, glorious and all-laudable apostles;
> of our father among the saints, John Chrysostom,
> Archbishop of Constantinople; [the saints of the
> locality and the day are mentioned];
> of the holy and righteous Ancestors of God,
> Joachim and Anna; and of all the saints:
> have mercy on us and save us,
> for He is good and loves mankind.

Commentary: *At every liturgy the holy gifts are*
fully consumed. If the priest is not assisted by a
deacon, he consumes the gifts after the final blessing
and veneration of the Cross.

The saints are mentioned in the final blessing, that
Christ may be merciful not only because of our prayers, but also because of the intercessions of the saints.
Our first advocate is the Mother of God, the most pure
Virgin Mary. In the final blessing local saints and the
saints of the day are also mentioned. Major feasts have
their own special blessings.

After the final blessing, the choir sings "Many years" for the patriarch, the archbishop and the local metropolitans, as well as for all Orthodox Christians:

> Protect, O Lord, our most holy
> Patriarch. . . ;
> our most blessed father Archbishop. . . ;
> our most blessed father Metropolitan. . . ;
> the brethren of this holy temple
> and all the members of the congregation,
> and all Orthodox Christians,
> and grant them many years.

As he pronounces the blessing, the priest blesses the people with the cross. The cross, symbol of sacrifice in perfect love and of conquering death, is inseparably linked to the Liturgy. Thus the faithful, at the conclusion of the Liturgy, kiss the cross which the priest holds in his hand. During this time, the deacon, the choirmaster, or some member of the congregation reads prayers of thanks for Communion.

Commentary: *When the Liturgy is finished and the prayers of thanksgiving have been read, the priests and deacons greet one another in the sanctuary. Referring to the reception of Communion, the greeter says: "For the soul's salvation and health of body!" "For the glory of God!," the others reply.*

The congregation, too, can greet one another in this way, but only after the service is completely finished. Immediately after Communion, it is important to direct one's whole attention to the songs and prayers of thanksgiving in the Liturgy.

Those who have not received Communion or who

do not join in the prayer of thanksgiving leave the church in silence.

Commentary: *The New Testament and church history indicate how frequently people went to Communion at different times.*

During Apostolic times, those who believed in God were "continuing daily with one accord in the temple, and breaking bread from house to house, they ate their food with gladness and simplicity of heart" (Acts 2:46).

The "Breaking of Bread" in accordance with the Lord's commandment, the Eucharist of early times, was celebrated in homes, but otherwise people still went to pray in the temple. Elsewhere the New Testament shows that the people gathered for the Breaking of Bread in particular, on the first day of the week, the day of Christ's Resurrection (Acts 20:7). This day on which the Eucharist was celebrated was called the Lord's Day (Didache 14:1), which is still the Greek name for Sunday (Kyriake — the day dedicated to the Lord.)

Naturally the Eucharist was also central to the church feasts, those held on the anniversary of the death of a martyr and on the "great feasts," which gradually developed.

In the fourth century it became the general custom to celebrate the Liturgy on Saturdays as well. But in some places the Communion service was held several times a week. Basil the Great testifies to this in a letter to the patrician Caesaria: "We take Communion four times each week — on Sunday, on Wednesday, on Friday, and on Saturday — but it would be most useful to do it every day and receive Christ's Body and Blood." (Letter 93).

In Rome and Spain it became the general custom to go to Communion every day.

When the Great Fast of Lent was established at the turn of the fifth century, the celebration of the Liturgy in Lent was restricted to Saturday and Sunday. However, the need for the faithful to receive Communion more than twice a week even during Lent led to the development of the Liturgy of the Presanctified Gifts, so that Communion would be possible on Wednesdays and Fridays as well.

In subsequent centuries, after Christianity had gained official status, the Christians' eagerness for frequent Communion weakened in both the East and the West. Various factors estranged the people from the altar. The custom of reading the eucharistic prayers "secretly" without the people hearing them became general in the eighth century. (Correspondingly, in the West, the so-called "silent" masses came into use.) Further, what few fragments of the prayers reached the ears of the people at the Liturgy were in an antiquated language which lagged by centuries the living language of the people. In areas where Greek was used, the Liturgy was celebrated (and still is) in a classical, almost Homeric Greek; and in some Slavic churches, the Liturgy is still heard in the Old Church Slavonic language (Old Bulgarian). Naturally, the ear can get accustomed to these church languages, but this does not guarantee precise understanding.

Furthermore, the visual contact between the people and the altar was broken when it became the custom to erect high iconostases.

The end-result of this development was the notion of the "responsibility" to receive Communion "at least once a year."

Indeed, devout believers have always received Communion more than once a year. But the general understanding that every Liturgy — including particularly the Liturgy of the Presanctified Gifts — is celebrated in order for people to partake of Communion has been virtually lost. Instead, a "liturgical piety" has arisen according to which, in certain local churches, special conditions for partaking of Communion were set, such as fasting for three days, or compulsory confession before every Communion. The effect of this pastoral care was that more and more people fulfilled this "duty" only once a year. At the same time, people easily acquired the notion that, if certain set conditions were fulfilled, one was "fit" to take part in Communion. It would have been, and would still be, well to remember what the blessed Cassian of Rome (360-435) teaches about this "fitness:"

> *"It is much better to receive them every Sunday for the healing of our infirmities, with that humility of heart whereby we believe and confess that we can never touch those Holy Mysteries worthily, than to be puffed up by foolish persuasion of heart and believe that at the year's end we are ready to receive them."*

Only at the beginning of the twentieth century did this state of spiritual anemia begin to be overcome as the result of a liturgical awakening. This began in the Western Church, but it also made Orthodox theologians look deep into their original roots, into the teachings of the Church Fathers and the liturgical practice of the early Church, where the principle stated by Bishop Irenaeus of Lyons was realized: "Our doctrine is in accordance with the Eucharist, and the Eucharist in turn confirms our doctrine" (Adv. Haer. *IV, 18*).

A pastoral letter from the bishops of the Finnish Orthodox Church in 1970 emphasizes the importance of continually going to Communion. Pointing to the practice of the Greek Church, it removes the requirement of Confession for those who go to Communion as often as possible, with the blessing of their father confessor.

THE LITURGY IN THE WORLD

The Liturgy has ended. The Eucharist has been celebrated at the thousands of altars throughout the world — wherever possible, believers have gathered to receive the "Bread of Heaven" and to drink of the "Cup of Life."

On the same final evening on which Jesus celebrated a secret Communion with His disciples, He made a farewell speech to them and prayed to His Father for them and for those who, through their words, believed in Him. He spoke of the believers and of the world, in which they would "have trouble."

In our own post-Christian time, the concept of "world" in the sense in which Christ used it can be felt very clearly. Lands which were originally Christian are now either officially atheist or are neutral towards religion. Faith is considered as a private affair for the citizens.

Centuries have passed since nations' leaders, in their speeches, openly stated that they believed in God, appealed for His help, or did something to glorify His Name.

Man has now officially and publicly forgotten God. Turning his back on God, he now looks after the affairs of the world by the power of his own genius.

The Creator, from His own essential nature, endowed man with self-awarness, creativity, and a free will.

And what do we see in practice? Separated from the will of God and indifferent to it, man's free will is transformed, as the result of pride, suspicion and hatred, into a world-destroying power which causes both man and nature to groan.

Is there no place from which we might expect something decisively new, which could alter the direction of this development?

What if we are looking for solutions in the wrong direction?

Perhaps it is to be found in what has been left behind!

It came as good news "to all the nations" — as the Gospel.

Its influence can still be felt in all that is really beautiful, good, and right.

The Gospel has not come to nothing. The Eucharist — whether celebrated secretly in the barracks of a concentration camp or in a gilded cathedral — contains the timeless presence of the new message. There indeed time loses its meaning in an intersection of past, present and future, in the way in which Christ is at the same time both the Lamb of God who has taken away the sins of the world and the King of Glory raised to the glory of the Father.

Just as the Christians at the time of the martyrs met their crucified but risen Lord in Communion, so Christians in our time, who are "in the world but not of the world," experience the Eucharist as the source of the power of their faith.

Again and again, this power is given to the weary traveler along God's way.

Thus the "new" is continuously new and fresh in this age "till He comes."

And until then, the Christian's walking in newness of life (Rom 6:4) is "from Liturgy to Liturgy," a perpetual longing for the Love Feast of the Kingdom of God.

Commentary: *It is natural that the importance of going to Communion be brought out in a book dealing with the Liturgy. Communion is indeed a living bond with the Church, a sign of membership in Christ's Body. In the directions for the spiritual life, both the cultivation of personal prayer and reception of Communion are regarded as essential. One spiritual director (Bishop Justin) writes:*

> *"Every real Christian must always remember that it is indispensable for him to be united with our Lord the Savior in his whole being. . . And the surest way to achieve this union with the Lord, next to communion of His Flesh and Blood, is the inner Jesus Prayer:"*

"Lord Jesus Christ, Son of God, have mercy on me."

The above advice, as well as much other counsel for the spiritual life, is contained in Valamo Monastery's book on the Jesus Prayer (The Art of Prayer *[Faber, 1966] 193). Among other Orthodox books dealing with the life of faith we may mention the following: Father John,* Christ Is in Our Midst *(St. Vladimir's Seminary Press, 1980); Waddell,* The Desert Fathers *(University of Michigan, 1957); Archbishop Paul of Finland,* The Faith We Hold *(St Vladimir's Seminary Press, 1980); Kallistos Ware,* The Power of the Name *(Fairacres, 1974);* The Way of a Pilgrim *(SPCK, 1965);* The Philokalia I-III *(Faber, 1979-1984); Kallistos Ware,* The Orthodox Way *(Mowbrays, 1979).*

O Christ, Thou great and holy Passover!
O Wisdom, Word and Power of God!
Grant that we may more perfectly
partake of Thee
in the unending Day of Thy Kingdom.

(from John of Damascus' Easter canon [eighth century])

APPENDIX

AN ORTHODOX AT THE LITURGY

At the Liturgy, when you see others going to Communion, do not join the group just because you do not want to look different from the others. Going to Communion always implies that you wish to do so and that you have already made the decision before going to church.

Let it be evident in some way in your life that you have this desire and longing to take part in Communion.

Think about going to Communion before the morning when you go to church. Pray for a right disposition, especially for the grace of repentance, so that before Communion you may sincerely confess yourself to be "the first of sinners."

As you prepare your spirit, prepare your body also, fasting completely on the morning of your Communion, not eating or drinking anything.* It is also good, if you are able, to do without the evening meal the night before. When you feel uncomfortable from doing this, transform your hunger to spiritual hunger and thirst and wait to be satisfied at the Eucharist and Holy Communion.

Before Communion, as you read your evening and morning prayers, add one or more extra prayers. The Liturgy itself contains a preparation for Communion, but it is important also to prepare yourself personally in your own place of prayer.

---

*The main rule is not to eat or drink anything in the morning before going to Communion. During Lent, if the Liturgy is celebrated in the evening, the same kind of preparation is made, with the complete fast beginning at midday. It should be remembered, however, that taking medicines prescribed for specific times is not breaking the fast; it is right to do everything necessary to have enough strength to go to church. It is permitted also to sit in church if strength does not permit standing. It is good to remember that Holy Communion is received for the healing not only of the soul but also of the body.

107

The Apostle gives clear instructions about this. He says to those preparing for Communion: "Let a man examine himself, and so let him eat of that bread and drink of that cup."

And again he warns: "Whoever eats this bread or drinks this cup of the Lord in an unworthy manner will be guilty of the body and blood of the Lord" (I Cor 11:28-29, 27). Of what does this self-examination consist?

If a serious sin is weighing upon you, go first to Confession and only then, with your father confessor's blessing, go to Communion also.

If you simply feel unworthy in every respect, do not hesitate. Holy Communion is precisely for such people. It is not for those who approach the holy Cup with self-satisfaction. Indeed Holy Communion is given "for the remission of sins and unto life everlasting."

Of course the self-examination of which the Apostle spoke is not limited only to preparation for Communion—in fact one always means to go to Communion. Self-examination is the ongoing process of checking the direction of one's life. Am I moving towards God or away from Him? What is my attitude towards my neighbors? Do I offend them? Do I wrong them? Is there Christian love in me or only pious superficiality?

If you notice something in yourself which needs correcting, but you do not succeed in this right away, do not be depressed about it or abstain from Communion, as long as you are repentant of your weakness. Will He who commanded us to forgive "seventy times seven times" not forgive you if you sincerely repent?

The faith that participation in the Holy Body and Blood of Christ will give you strength will be realized in the improvements which you make. The Apostle gives comfort and hope, saying: "It is God who works in you both to will and to work" (Phil 2:13). And God works in you when you are sufficiently humbled and call on Him for help.

PRAYERS IN PREPARATION
FOR HOLY COMMUNION

to be read at home before going to church*

Morning Prayer

Arising from sleep I thank Thee, O Holy Trinity, that, of Thy great kindness and long-suffering, Thou hast not had indignation against me, for I am slothful and sinful, neither hast Thou destroyed me in my transgressions: but Thou hast shown Thy customary love towards man, and hast raised me up as I lay in heedlessness, that I might sing my morning hymn and glorify Thy sovereignty. Do Thou now enlighten the eyes of my understanding, open my ears to receive Thy words and teach me Thy commandments. Help me to do Thy will, to hymn Thee, to confess Thee from my heart, and to extol Thine All-holy Name, of Father, Son and Holy Spirit, now and ever, and unto ages of ages. Amen.

O come, let us worship God our King.
O come, let us worship and fall down before Christ, our King and our God.
O come, let us worship and fall down before Christ Himself, our King and our God.

Psalm
116

I believed, therefore I spoke,
'I am greatly afflicted.'
I said in my haste
'All men are liars.'

What shall I render to the Lord
For all His benefits towards me?
I will take up the cup of salvation,
And call upon the Name of the Lord.

A person who is accustomed to preparing for Communion by reading prayers from the Orthodox prayer book will naturally continue to do so. Lacking such a prayer book, one can very well use the prayers given here. What is most important is not the number of prayers but the humility and faith with which they are read.

I will pay my vows to the Lord
Now in the presence of all His people.

Precious in the sight of the Lord
Is the death of His saints.
O Lord, truly I am Thy servant;
I am Thy servant, the son of Thy maidservant;
Thou hast loosed my bonds.
I will offer to Thee the sacrifice of thanksgiving,
And will call upon the Name of the Lord.

I will pay my vows to the Lord
Now in the presence of all His people,
In the courts of the Lord's house,
In the midst of you, O Jerusalem.

Praise the Lord!

Glory to the Father, and to the Son, and
    to the Holy Spirit
Now and ever and unto ages of ages. Amen.

Alleluia! Alleluia! Alleluia!
Glory to Thee, O Lord, glory to Thee.
Glory to Thee, O Lord, glory to Thee.
Glory to Thee, O Lord, glory to Thee.

Lord, have mercy. Lord, have mercy.
    Lord, have mercy.

Troparia O Lord, born of the Virgin,
regard not my transgressions:
cleanse Thou my heart,
and make of it a temple
for Thy most pure Body and Thy Blood:
cast me not away from Thy presence,
Thou who hast mercy without measure.

Glory to the Father, and to the Son, and
    to the Holy Spirit.

How dare I take of Thy hallowed things,
unworthy as I am?

For if I make bold to draw nigh unto Thee
among them that are worthy,
and it appears that I have no wedding garment,
I do but procure the condemnation
of my sinful soul:
cleanse my defiled soul, O Lord, and save me,
for Thou art the lover of mankind.

Now and ever and unto ages of ages. Amen.

Great is the multitude of my transgressions,
O Mother of God:
unto Thy purity I have recourse, seeking
    salvation:
visit my soul in my infirmity,
and pray thy Son our God to grant me
the remission of my evil deeds,
Thou who alone art blessed.

Prayers of St. John Chrysostom

First prayer

I am not worthy, Master and Lord,
that Thou shouldst enter under the roof of my
    soul;
yet inasmuch as Thou desirest to live in me
as the Lover of men, I approach with boldness.
Thou hast commanded: Let the doors be
opened which Thou Thyself alone hast made
and Thou shalt enter with Thy love for men
just as Thou art.

Thou shalt enter and enlighten my darkened
reasoning. I believe that Thou wilt do this.
For Thou didst not cast away the prostitute
who came to Thee with tears,
neither didst Thou turn away
the tax-collector who repented,
nor didst Thou reject the thief
who acknowledged Thy kingdom,
nor didst Thou forsake the repentent persecutor,
the Apostle Paul, even as he was.

But all who came to Thee in repentance
Thou didst unite to the ranks of Thy friends,
who alone art blessed forever,
now and unto the endless ages. Amen.

Second prayer

I believe, O Lord, and I confess
that Thou art truly the Christ
the Son of the living God
who camest into the world to save sinners,
of whom I am first. I believe also
that this is truly Thine own most pure Body,
and that this is truly Thine own precious Blood.
Therefore, I pray Thee: have mercy upon me
and forgive my transgressions
both voluntary and involuntary, of word and
    of deed,
committed in knowledge or in ignorance.
And make me worthy to partake without
    condemnation
of Thy most pure Mysteries,
for the remission of my sins, and unto life
    everlasting.
Amen.

Of Thy Mystical Supper, O Son of God,
accept me today as a communicant;
for I will not speak of Thy Mystery to Thine
    enemies,
neither like Judas will I give Thee a kiss;
but like the thief will I confess Thee;
Remember me, O Lord, in Thy kingdom.

May the communion of Thy holy Mysteries
be neither to my judgment, nor to my
    condemnation,
O Lord, but to the healing of soul and body.